Provincial flags of Ontario and Québec

HELLO OTTAWA
Canada's National Capital 2022-23
In Full Color

CONTENTS

DETAILED MAPS: In a book that is 8.5 x 11 inches or even smaller in Kindle format, it is impossible to provide really good, detailed maps. The maps I have used in this book are from OpenStreetMap.com, a free web site that enables you to zoom into any city or region and find exceptional detail. Rather than fill up pages in my book with maps that are so easily obtained on line and can actually be used on a Smart Phone when you are traveling, I have just provided a few basic maps to illustrate the points I need to make in the various chapters.

The Canadian Coat of Arms

WELCOME TO CANADA – BONJOUR A CANADA

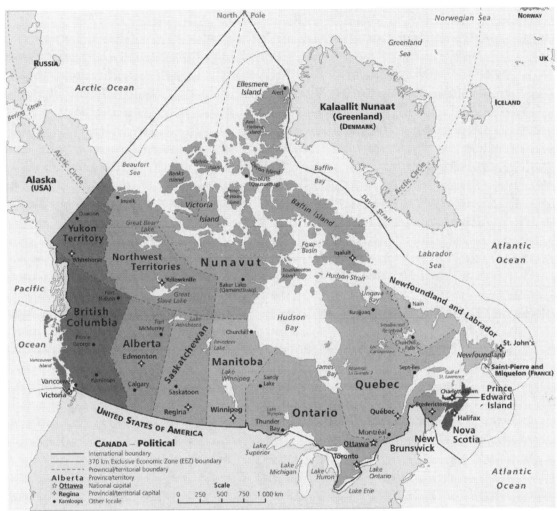

The Provinces and Territories of Canada

In physical size Canada is the second largest nation on earth. In size, it is second only to Russia with 9,976,085 square kilometers or 3,851,787 square miles. If you look at the North American continent, you will notice that it continues to widen as you move north. Thus to cross Canada by road or rail entails a longer journey than crossing the United States. Whitehorse in the Yukon Territory is over 1,126 kilometers or 700 miles farther west than San Francisco while St. John's, Newfoundland is nearly 1,609 kilometers or 1,000 miles farther east than Boston. This greater expanse gives Canada two more time zones than the lower 48 states.

There is an illustrative story in Canada regarding its size. According to the story, a young man living in Vancouver (on the Pacific coast) receives a telegram from his father saying, "Son your brother is coming to visit you. His flight arrives in St. John's on Saturday. Please pick him up at the airport." Now St. John's is the capital of Newfoundland (on the far Atlantic coast). Of course the parents are not aware of the fact that it is over 8,050 kilometers or 5,000 miles east of Vancouver. So the son writes back via e-mail, "Dear dad, you pick him up since you are closer." St. John's is 1,609 kilometers or 1,000 miles closer to London than it is to Vancouver. This anecdote may give you some appreciation of the size and scope of Canada.

Unlike the United States, Canada is an empty land, often called "The Great White North" because of its long, cold winters. With a population of approximately 36,286,000, Canada has an average density of 3,6 per square kilometer or 9.4 people per square mile. With 324,227,000 people and 9,826,629 square kilometers or 3,794,083 square miles, the population density of the United States is 32.99 per square kilometer or 85.4 people per square mile, and this includes the vast emptiness of Alaska, so it is clear that Canadians have a lot more legroom than does the United States. As a Canadian, this is something to feel good about, knowing our country is so fast and still has so much unspoiled land out there even though most of us never explore it.

Despite the fact that Canada has so much legroom, most Canadians live in the major cities of the country, the majority of which are less than a day's drive from the American border. Some "wise guy" American once said that if the border were not there, most Canadians would be living even farther south. He must have been from Florida, as his reference was to the intense cold of the northern winters without regard for the hundreds of years of history and the pride in our culture that we Canadians have.

Ottawa is located within the province of Ontario, but situated on the south bank of the Ottawa River across from Hull-Gatineau, Québec. The most direct route from Ottawa south to the nearest border crossing into the United States is 81 kilometers or 50 miles at Ogdensburg, New York on the St. Lawrence River.

Even though winter can be brutal, we Canadians love our land and most would not choose to live in the United States, although we do envy those who live in Florida or Arizona during the winter months. And many do spend the winter months south of the border in either Florida or Arizona, but that is only an interlude, as most Canadians would not want to live permanently in the United States. They are two different countries with two distinctly different lifestyles, so for Canadians living in the United States or for Americans living in Canada requires quite an adjustment.

This book will focus upon greater Ottawa which is Canada's fourth largest metropolis a very popular summer destination for American visitors because of it being the national capital. Toronto is, however, still the provincial capital and the financial hub of the nation. In many ways they are rival cities.

This is not a travel guide similar to Frommers, but rather an introduction to Ottawa and its surroundings relative to geography, history and culture. It does provide many recommendations for accommodation and dining, but only those establishments that are highly rated. I like to call it a bit of "snob appeal." This book will in the end make you a more "savvy" visitor, giving you valuable background regarding this awesome urban center, especially its cultural patterns, which differ from the other major cities of Canada.

But before we look at Ottawa, it is first essential to talk in broad terms about the basic geography and history of Canada. So many potential visitors, especially those from the United States and Western Europe, have little or no knowledge of the scope of Canada and its strong cultural dichotomy between the English and French speaking areas. Nor do most people have a grasp of Canadian history. Visiting Halifax and Sydney without having this understanding limits your capability to truly get to know this city and its people within the context of the nation. Canada may share the same landmass as the United States, but it lies to the north and also possesses many landscape features not found in its neighbor to the south. Historically this is a country with a deeply rooted French cultural background that was conquered by the British and ultimately developed two distinct personalities.

The government's passport stamp of welcome

CANADA
THE NATURAL LANDSCAPE

THE LANDSCAPE: Many of the landscape features of the United States extend north into Canada. Canada shares the Pacific Coast Mountains, the intermountain plateaus, Rocky Mountains and Prairies with the United States. And along the eastern margin of the country you find the Appalachian Mountains extending all the way into the Atlantic Provinces. But there are some distinct differences. The Pacific Coast Mountains reach their maximum elevations within Canada, topping out at 5,959 meters or 19,551 feet, making it one of the highest mountain ranges of the entire continent. The intermountain plateaus are much colder than those in the United States, and they are marginally semi-arid, but with scattered groves of pine and willow. And they contain numerous large glacial lakes.

In the Pacific Coast Mountains of northern British Columbia

The Canadian Rocky Mountains are composed of sedimentary rock that was heavily sculpted by glacial ice and appear similar to the Alps of Europe with dramatic peaks unlike the American Rockies. In Canada the Great Plains are known as the Prairies. They contain a combination of grassland mixed with woodland and are also dotted with glacial lakes. So yes we share many geographic zones that are the same, but visually the natural Canadian landscapes are quite different from their southern counterpart.

Above the Great Lakes the country is dominated over by the hard rock Canadian Shield, a vast region covered in thick forest and dotted with around a million lakes that result from the scour of the glaciers of the last Ice Age. The Great Lakes, shared by both countries, drain through the valley of the St. Lawrence River, which forms the heartland of the province of Québec. Most of the land in Québec lies within the Canadian Shield, but the vast majority of its nearly 9,000,000 residents live in the St. Lawrence River Valley or on the margins of the Appalachian Mountains to the east of the river. Many large tributaries drain off the Canadian Shield into the St. Lawrence. To the east of the river, the Atlantic Provinces are essentially a part of the ancient Appalachian Mountain chain extending north to the Gulf of St. Lawrence and the landscapes are a continuation of those seen in the American state of Maine.

Approaching the Rocky Mountains from the prairies of Alberta

Unlike the bulk of the United States, nearly all of Canada experiences harsh winters with snow covering the land. Of all the provinces, Québec often receives some of the heaviest snowfall in the nation. It was near Montréal in the early 1900's that a Monsieur Bombardier had become so fed up with the state of the roads in winter that he invented a vehicle that could tackle them - today we know it as the snowmobile. Winters are also very severe in the Prairie Provinces of the interior. Only the Pacific Coast fringe has a milder, yet very wet maritime climate not unlike that of England. But the snow level hovers just a few hundred meters above sea level. The Atlantic Coast can be subjected to extreme gale force storms from Newfoundland to Nova Scotia, often with equally heavy snowfall.

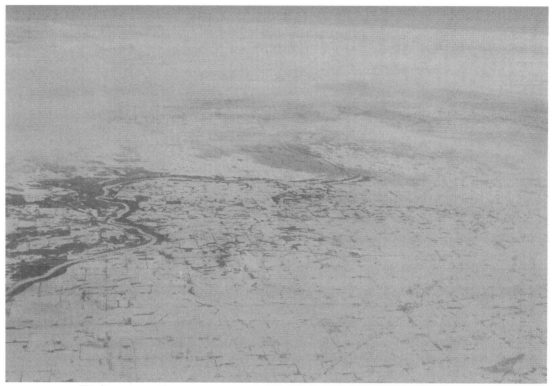

Flying over the snow covered Prairies of Alberta in January

POLITICAL DIVISIONS: Canada is divided into ten provinces and three federal territories. A Canadian province is like a state, but it has a greater degree of internal autonomy and more political clout than an American states. For example, provinces can negotiate directly with foreign governments regarding the development of resources; they have a total say in the development of health care programs and they own most of the land within their boundaries whereas in the United States, most land that is not privately owned is federal land. Just as in the United States, a Canadian province has a capital city, issues its own license plates and is well marked with large welcome signs along its borders. Most of the provinces are much larger than their American counterpart states because they are fewer in number. Of all the provinces, only Québec has been given special accord to develop many of its institutions along strictly French cultural lines, and even imposing the French language as the only officially recognized language in the province. In a way it is like a country within a country. Alberta, Manitoba and New Brunswick however, do have moderately significant French speaking populations originally resulting from early French settlers in the east and fur trappers out west.

The gentle countryside of southern Ontario

Autumn along the St. Lawrence River in Québec

The west coast of Newfoundland in summer

The rugged eastern coast of Newfoundland in late summer

What about our national capital city? Canada's national capital straddles the border between the provinces of Ontario and Québec. The main seat of government is in the city of Ottawa, Ontario, however, many important government offices are located across the Ottawa River in the sister city of Hull-Gatineau, Québec. As a nation that is bicultural and bilingual, the location of the national capital was deliberate, chosen in 1867 by Her Majesty Queen Victoria to be a center that would bind the two primary cultures together. And over the years since independence, it truly has become the most bilingual city in the nation. Visually its public architecture is strongly influenced by British Gothic style and gives you the feeling of being in the British Isles.

Parliament Hill in Ottawa seen from Gatineau, Québec

THE CANADIAN CHARACTER

The history of any nation tells us much about the present day landscapes and the cultural makeup of the people. Canada has a rich and colorful history, one that has interacted with that of the United States on several occasions, but by in large, has evolved on its own. It is the history of Canada that gives the nation its distinct qualities and makes it a very different country from its neighbor to the south. Understanding this history enables a visitor to Calgary to better understand the visual landscape and the local culture with its distinct customs and flavors. So even if history is not your favorite subject, please read the rest of this chapter carefully so you can come to Ottawa or other parts of Canada and say to others, "Yes I do understand Canadian history and I even know how your government functions." It is nice to be a "savvy" tourist.

French farmers and fishermen are the original European settlers of the St. Lawrence River and the Gaspé Peninsula, which became the core of French North America. They also settled in what would later become New Brunswick and Nova Scotia, then known as Acadia. Their first capital of Port-Royal dates back to 1605, which is three years before the creation of Ville de Québec in 1608. Most Canadian history timelines show the French initially settling Canada in 1608, 12 years before the Pilgrims landed at Plymouth Rock. Ville de Québec was the first settlement, founded by Samuel de Champlain and built on a high bluff overlooking the St. Lawrence River. It is now the oldest and most historic city in Canada. But French colonists were not very willing for the most part to come to New France, as it was a harsh land unlike the milder and more fertile English colonies being established to the south. Farming was difficult and most settlers struggled to be successful. Fur trapping and exploring became important elements of the culture and many French fur trappers explored well west into the prairies and Rocky Mountains, often settling in Native American villages.

Montréal was the second major colony established in 1642 at the head of navigation on the St. Lawrence River. The name is a contraction of the two French words for Mount Royal as the settlement was built at the base of a forested mountain on an island in the river from which sentries could watch the entire surrounding countryside for native or British intrusion. This was as far as boats could navigate the river without being taken out to portage around the Lachine Rapids. When Jacques Cartier explored the river, he at first thought he had found the elusive Northwest Passage that would take him to Asia, thus the name Lachine, which translates to China Rapids. The real Northwest Passage is today a reality, but it is so far to the north, located between the many islands in the Arctic Ocean. During summer you can even take a cruise now between Nome, Alaska and New York via the Arctic that is if you have around $50,000 per person you are willing to spend.

French explorers and trappers ventured out into the Great Lakes country and down the Mississippi River to the Gulf of Mexico, claiming all of the land for King Louis XIV, thus the name Louisiana. Other explorers ventured west into the Prairies as far as the Rocky Mountains by 1748. Although agricultural settlement was limited, and by 1760, there were only 60,000 settlers in Québec, the influence of the French was significant as trappers, known as voyageurs, established regular trade contacts with tribes all across this immense region. Some even lived among the tribes, taking native wives. It is somewhat of a romantic saga of early Canadian history, but in reality it was a hard life.

The British attempted to box in French colonial holdings by establishing a fur-trading company in the Hudson Bay region in 1670, and in the early 18th century by seizing the Atlantic colony of Acadia in 1710, later guaranteed by a peace treaty in 1713. As the British gained control of Acadia (present day New Brunswick and Nova Scotia), the French colonists were evicted. Many fled south to the newly established French colony of New Orleans and are known today as Cajun, a corruption of the original name Acadian. The dialect of French spoken in the Bayous of Louisiana is very similar to that spoken in Québec today. The French retained control of Cape Breton Island and established a large fortress at Louisbourg to protect their access to the St. Lawrence against further British aggression, but in 1758 it ultimately fell to the British. But even now the music and some of the slang you hear in the far north of Nova Scotia have a tie to the Acadian culture.

During this same period, the British were becoming well established in what would grow to be the 13 Colonies along the Atlantic seaboard. Where the two spheres of influence met in the Appalachian Mountains, both the French and British attempted to ally various native tribes, which ultimately led to conflict over the vast Ohio River territories. Essentially the French were more successful in gaining the support of the Native American tribes because they had a less superior attitude when dealing with native peoples than did the British.

The ultimate war that developed between the French and the British is one event shared in the history of both the United States and Canada. As tensions ultimately led to war, the result for France was the loss of its most important colony, Québec. The war lasted from 1754 to 1763, with campaigns being fought from the Ohio River to Cape Breton Island, as well as battles in the Caribbean, North Africa and Europe itself. This was more than just a war for the valley of the St. Lawrence; it was a contest between two great powers over the future control of the interior of North America.

The most noted battle of the war was that over the great fortress protecting Ville de Québec. Two important generals, Wolfe and Montcalm were pitted against each other in a siege on the fortress of Québec during the fall of 1758, which culminated in a battle on the Plains of Abraham outside of the impregnable fortress. The British managed to draw the French forces out of their stronghold. Neither general lived to see the battle concluded, but the British were the ultimate victors. However, the following spring, the French Canadian militia drew out the British forces and handed them a major defeat. But as a British flotilla of ships arrived in May 1760, the French Canadian forces withdrew to Montréal. But rather than risking another conflict in which innocent civilians would be killed, the governor surrendered on September 8, 1760. Although the British now occupied the two key cities of the St. Lawrence, the war did not end until 1763, when a treaty concluded hostilities.

The British government inherited a vast colonial territory with over 60,000 French subjects who were now cut off from their homeland. In a gesture of magnanimity the French people were allowed to maintain their language, customs and religion intact without interference from British authorities. This was a first time concession by the British. Little did they know what that gesture would mean in the future history of Canada. Had such rights not been granted to the French, Canada today would not have its distinct dual cultural and linguistic heritage, which has been both a joy at times and a curse at other times.

To keep from losing their vast Louisiana holdings to the British, France gave control of the territory to Spain, only to later receive the territory back at the time of the American Revolution. And since it was too costly to maintain, the French ultimately sold Louisiana to the new United States in 1803.

The colony of Québec changed drastically at the time of the American Revolution. Prior to 1776, there were a handful of British subjects living in the St. Lawrence Valley, primarily government officials and soldiers. They did not interact with the French colonists, thus Québec maintained its distinctly French flavor. When the Declaration of Independence was issued and the 13 Colonies began to prepare for war, British Loyalists knew that their lives would be in danger if they remained. A mass exodus of over 40,000 fled to the British held territories to the north, primarily into Nova Scotia, but some 7,000 chose to carve out a new home on the northern shores of Lake Erie and Lake Ontario in the region of Québec that was unsettled. Thus the bicultural seed for Canada was sewn as now there were settlers representing two cultures and languages.

In 1791, the colony of Québec was divided into two separate colonies to enable each culture to exist in its own territory. The English dominated area around the Great Lakes became known as Upper Canada, while Québec was renamed Lower Canada. By the first decade of the 19th century, Upper Canada had a population of over 80,000, most having come from the United States, claiming to be Loyalists, although some were just eager to seek out new lands for settlement.

Conflicts over the border between the new United States and the British along with British harassment of American ships at sea led to the War of 1812, and this worried British officials as much of the population of Upper Canada claimed to be loyal to the Crown, but their pledges had yet to be tested. The war dragged on into 1814 when both sides agreed to a declaration of peace. In actuality, the war was a stalemate as neither side could claim victory. But events left their mark for years to come. British forces had invaded Washington, burning the White House and other government buildings. In retaliation, American forces burned Fort York (present day Toronto), an event that is still taught in Canadian schools as an act of great audacity. "How dare those Yankees coming north and burning our city." It's all in the point of view because it was we, or should I say British troops, who first burned Washington.

In 1840, Upper and Lower Canada were unified, an event that turned out to be unsuccessful as the English and French politicians could not agree on issues, literally paralyzing the colonial government. The union was broken and when the two colonies reemerged, the names Ontario and Québec become recognized. Many historians have argued that the motivation for creating one colony with its English and French components was to eventually swamp the Francophone populace and ultimately force both the English language and British ways upon the Québécois and dissolve their cultural unity. In the end, however, it did not work.

By 1850, immigration to the Canadian colonies had swelled the population to nearly 2,000,000, primarily from the British Isles, thus English-speaking people began to outnumber the French, despite the higher French Canadian birth rate. Montréal became the primary shipping and manufacturing hub of the colonies, especially since American goods shipped to Britain via Canada could enter the mother country free of duty. This helped to give Canadian merchants an edge, fostering a booming economy. Although Québec was still predominantly French in culture, English-speaking businessmen heavily dominated its economic affairs.

The American Civil War had a drastic impact upon the future of Canada. In 1862, the United States and Britain almost went to war when a Union warship stopped a British vessel to remove two Confederate diplomats en route to London. This so outraged the British that they sent reinforcements to Canada. In 1864, Confederate raiders attacked St. Albans, Vermont via Québec, and despite being later captured by British forces, they were set free to the dismay of American settlers living along the border. Other such incidents only served to inflame public opinion in the United States.

At the end of the American Civil War, the economic reciprocity agreement that had existed between the Canadian colonies and the United States was not renewed, primarily as retaliation for Britain's apparent Confederate sympathies and attempts at running the Union blockade of the southern states. This forced Canadians to begin looking inward and attempt to build upon their own strengths. The difficulty was of course the great distances and the lack of any railway connections to the Pacific where the colony of British Columbia was slowly developing. West of the Great Lakes the land was still unsettled across the Prairies.

There were minor settlements in British Columbia and the potential was there for greater development of its storehouse of natural resources, but it was thousands of uncharted kilometers away with no link to the east, with much wild land in between.

In the United States, there had been pre Civil War agitation to fight the British to settle the western border at 54 degrees 40 minutes north latitude, but in 1849, a compromise was reached that set the border at the 49th parallel of latitude from Lake of the Woods to the shores of Puget Sound. Now at the end of the War, there was agitation in the American Congress to annex all of Canada, which would have meant a war with the British. But given the fever of "Manifest Destiny," there were many in the American government willing to risk such a war.

Since 1864, representatives of the Canadian colonies had held various meetings on the possibility of creating a confederation. Under the threat of American invasion, the meetings took on a new meaning. At Charlottetown, Prince Edward Island, agreement was reached on a confederation, and in 1867, the British Parliament passed the British North America Act, creating the Dominion of Canada. This was the first time in the history of the British Empire that independence was voluntarily granted to a grouping of colonies. By enabling independence, the British government removed the threat of a United States takeover. An invasion of a sovereign nation would have brought the Americans condemnation from the world community.

The newly formed Canada did not include all of what we see today. Initially, the confederation consisted of only the lower portions of Ontario, Québec plus New Brunswick and Nova Scotia. Prince Edward Island, Newfoundland and British Columbia chose to stay apart from the new nation, remaining as British colonies. The three Prairie Provinces had as yet not even come into existence. Thus the vast Prairie region and the west remained in the hands of the British, most of it being administered by the Hudson's Bay Company. Under the British North America Act, Canada was created as a bicultural and bilingual nation, but in reality it would not be until the 1960's when the true meaning of this act would come to fruition.

To solidify relations between the French and English peoples, Queen Victoria selected the site of Ottawa to be the national capital, as it was situated along the Ottawa River with Québec located on the opposite side. As the national capital has grown, its suburbs have spilled over into Québec.

At the time of Canadian confederation, the west was an empty wilderness containing only some 15,000 settlers, mainly of mixed blood, combining French and Native American, known as the Métis. The Métis were concentrated primarily along the banks of the Red River in what is today Manitoba. In 1869, Canada purchased the land that is Manitoba from the Hudson's Bay Company for $1,500,000. A later purchase added the entire Hudson's Bay Company territory, extending westward from Manitoba to British Columbia and northward to the shores of the Arctic Ocean. In landmass, these acquisitions made Canada the second largest nation on earth, a title it still holds to this day. The Métis were uncertain as to Canadian intentions, thus they rebelled against the takeover. Under the leadership of Louis Riel, they seized Fort Garry, the Hudson's Bay Company outpost. Their terms for union with Canada were guarantees for protection of the French culture, language and religion, terms that the federal government initially agreed to negotiate. One unfortunate incident in which Riel ordered the execution of a settler of British descent, ultimately forced the Canadian prime minister to send in troops to guarantee public safety during the negotiations. Louis Riel escaped, but the Métis were granted their terms and in 1870, Manitoba joined Canada as a province. In later years Louis Riel led a major revolt by the Métis, only it was crushed and he was captured, tried and executed as a traitor. But today in Manitoba he is considered to be a folk hero and there is even a statue of him in front of the provincial legislature building. Manitoba is the only other province outside of Québec where there is a significant French speaking population, especially in and around the city of Winnipeg.

Unlike the Wild West of the American Frontier, the Canadian government negotiated treaties with the Native American tribes of the Prairies and Rocky Mountains, guaranteeing reservations, schools, cash payments and tools in exchange for the vast tracts of land the natives once roamed.

To insure law and order in the west as settlers moved out onto the Prairies, the government established the North West Mounted Police in 1873, today better known as the Royal Canadian Mounted Police. Their role was critical in the settlement of both Alberta and Saskatchewan, which gained provincial status in 1905. By adhering to treaty agreements and through vigilant enforcement of the law by the Mounties, Canada was spared the intense bloodshed that characterized the American expansion into the Great Plains and far western regions. The Mounties earned the respect of Native American and White Men alike for their diligence. Even today in a world where police are often taunted or maligned by many in the community, in Canada there is great respect for the RCMP, or better known simply as the Mounties. And yes the scarlet red coat is worn, but only for special dress occasions. And most Mounties are trained to ride horseback.

British Columbia, a colony rich in minerals, timber and fish, was reluctant to join the Canadian confederation, given the distance between the west coast and Manitoba, which was the nearest Canadian province. Their price was a guarantee of a transcontinental railroad. In 1871, British Columbia joined confederation and work began on the building of the Canadian Pacific Railroad. The line opened in 1885, connecting Vancouver with the east. This not only tied the expanding nation together, but it opened up the Prairies for settlement. By 1905, Saskatchewan and Alberta had sufficient population to become provinces. The railroad was built by a private company, but heavily subsidized in land grants and capital by the federal government. In later years, the government itself entered into competition with Canadian Pacific, developing the Canadian National Railway system, which extended a transcontinental line west to Prince Rupert on the northern British Columbia coast, with an additional line southwest to Vancouver.

Great cattle ranches in Alberta in the early 20th century

Prince Edward Island, which had hosted the important confederation conference, held out on joining Canada until 1973. Newfoundland, on the other hand, refused to become a part of Canada, remaining as a British colony until 1949. After World War II, the British government forced a referendum upon the people of Newfoundland, the end result being union with Canada. To this day, there are people in the province who claim that the British rigged the election in favor of confederation as most Newfoundlanders either wanted to remain as a British colony or gain total independence. Many older "Newfies" still feel they were cheated and they think of their province as if it were a country.

The final acts in total national status occurred during the 20th century. In 1931, British Parliament passed the Statutes of Westminster. In this act, the British government removed its final veto power over the Canadian Parliament, thus giving the nation its complete sovereign status. This action would also apply to the other newly formed Commonwealth nations, as they gained their independence. However, since 1867, the Canadian people have, by their own choice, retained a tie to the monarchy. Canada accepted Queen Victoria and all her future heirs as the head of state of the nation under the title King or Queen of Canada. Despite the Statutes of Westminster granting full autonomy to the Canadian people, by choice the Crown is still the titular head of the government, but represented by a prominent Canadian citizen functioning as the Governor General. . In 1982, the Canadian Government had the physical document of the British North America Act brought to Canada from its prior home in Westminster, seat of British power.

Today there are movements to disengage from the Crown in several countries that have maintained a tie to the Royal Family. In 2021 Barbados disengaged and others are seriously considering it. Canada is not among them.

The Charter of Freedoms was added under the Constitution Act, and over the ensuing years, several amendments have been made. In combination, the Act, the Charter and the amendments form the Canadian Constitution, but it is not one single document like that of the United States.

THE GOVERNMENT AND ITS FUNCTION: When visiting Toronto, Vancouver, Halifax or any other city in Canada, it is difficult to watch the news on television or read a newspaper and fully understand the stories relating to the actions of the Canadian or local government. The entire system of governing Canada is based upon the British parliamentary system. To help in better appreciating how different Canada is from its southern neighbor, this section explains the terminology and the actual functions of the Canadian government. Thus when you are in Canada, you will be able to understand something of what is happening within the country politically. And it is quite fascinating because of its more Old World flavor.

Her Majesty Elizabeth II, Queen of Canada (Work of Joel Rouse, Ministry of Defence, Open Government License V3.0)

* THE CROWN: The head of state for Canada is Her Majesty, Elizabeth II, Queen of Canada. However, since the queen cannot live in Canada and the 15 other

nations within the British Commonwealth of Nations that have voluntarily accepted the Crown, a representative is chosen by the Canadian Government to act on the queen's behalf. This individual is selected for a five-year term, normally from the ranks of prominent citizens, and is known as the Governor General.

The Governor General is the physical embodiment of Queen Elizabeth, serving in all official capacities where the queen would normally function. The Governor General has the ultimate power of veto over the parliament, and in the event of a deadlock within the legislative body, has the power to call for a national election. The present Governor General of Canada is Her Excellency Mary Mae Simon, the first governor general to be of indigenous ethnic origin. She is now a major symbol of the importance of recognizing the native heritage of Canada's original citizens.

The Right Honourable Mary May Simon, Governor General

* **PARLIAMENT:** A legislative body known as the Canadian Parliament governs Canada. It is divided into two houses, and patterned after the British Parliament.

* **The Senate:** This body is composed of Senators who are appointed rather than elected. There are 107 seats in the Senate apportioned by province on the basis of population. It is primarily a reviewing body and the members are prominent citizens, selected for their contributions to the nation. The ruling party in the lower house names new senators when vacancies occur. Members normally served for life, today must retire at age 75. Senators represent the various political parties of the nation, and debates are conducted according to the same rules as in the lower house (to be discussed below). The function of the Senate, like the House of Lords in Britain is to review legislation passed by the lower house and make recommendations to the Governor General with regard to giving royal assent or

issuing a veto. There are limited occasions when the Senate may initiate legislation with regard to the welfare of the people of Canada so long as the bill does not involve taxation. The Senate may also form special committees to investigate matters that could lead to new legislation.

* The House of Commons or Lower House: This is the primary body of the parliament. Although it is called the lower house, it is where the power of government rests. Just as in the British Parliament, the House of Commons represents the people. There are 338 seats, apportioned by province on the basis of population with Ontario and Québec dominating because of their populations. After each national census, the seats are reapportioned and the number of seats may be increased to enable each member to represent approximately the same number of people from the district they serve. Districts are known as Ridings. The member representing a riding is known as a Member of Parliament or abbreviated as "MP."

The Right Honourable Justin Trudeau, Prime Minister of Canada

* POLITICAL PARTIES: At present, Canada has four major political parties that are represented in the House of Commons.

* Liberal Party: The Canadian Liberal Party is similar in its outlook to the Democratic Party in the United States. This party supports labor, is strongly oriented toward an effective welfare net for the public and tends to favor the role of larger government. It had been the party in power in the House of Commons continuously since 1991, but lost in 2006. They regained power in 2015.

* Canadian Conservative Party: This is essentially a new party that was created in November 2003 after a long rift in the Canadian right. When the Progressive Conservative Party lost the election of 1991 in a resounding defeat, the more right wing Canadian Reform Party came to dominance as the primary representative body for the conservative political right. However, neither the Reform (later renamed the Canadian Alliance) nor the Progressive Conservatives alone could win a national election over the Liberals. Thus they decided to merge in 2003 to reunite the right. They came back into power in 2006, first as a minority government, winning again as a minority government in 2008 and finally becoming a majority governing party in 2011. But in a surprising upset, they lost to the Liberal Party in the fall election of 2015. Justin Trudeau, the son of the late Pierre Trudeau, who served as Prime Minister longer than anyone in Canadian history, now leads the Liberal Party as Prime Minister. His good looks and charm have captivated many Canadians and people abroad as well. In 2017 when he visited Japan for the G7 Meeting, the Japanese teens were calling him the "Hunky Prime Minister."

Confederation Hall in Charlottetown, Prince Edward Island where four colonies agreed to the creation of Canada in 1867.

* New Democratic Party: This is a party that has represented a more socialistic viewpoint on the left. It originated in the Prairie Provinces and has had strong support from the agricultural sector of the economy. Although it has won various provincial elections, it has not been strong enough to win a national election. But in the 2011 election, it gained the second highest number of seats and headed up Her Majesty's Loyal Opposition until the 2015 election.

* Bloc Québécois: This party has represented the separatist movement within the province of Québec. Given that Québec is the second most populated province, thus having a large number of seats in the House of Commons, the Bloc has from time to time been a significant force politically. The issue of separatism for Québec has been laid to rest, as the province has received special recognition status and in many ways governs its internal affairs as a nation within a nation. In the 2011 election, the Bloc won only two seats, and it did not do well in the 2015 election either, as its power had been predicated upon agitation for separation, a topic presently put to bed.

* NATIONAL ELECTIONS: National elections must be held once every five years at the maximum, but can be held at any time within three years of coming to power when the ruling party chooses to call one, or in the event of a deadlock in the debates of the House of Commons when at least 51 percent of the members vote no confidence in the ruling party. Once the Governor General calls for a national election, approximately six weeks are allowed for campaigning prior to the vote. However, in the 2015 election the then Prime Minister insisted on an 11-week period, which actually served to his party's detriment. Citizens will vote in their respective Riding for the candidate who represents the party they wish to see rule. During the campaign period, the leader of each party is the person whom most media attention focuses upon.

Once the votes are counted, the party that receives the greatest number of votes is then called upon by the Governor General to form a government. This means that the party leader will become the Prime Minister. He or she will then designate top ranking party members to hold the portfolios of the various government ministries such as external affairs, defense, labor, etc. These members then comprise the cabinet and along with the Prime Minister they represent The Government.

The opposition parties collectively constitute Her Majesty's Loyal Opposition and the leader of the party with the second highest number of seats becomes the Leader of the Opposition. His or her role is to challenge the party in power at every turn, thus representing those citizens who did not vote for the party now holding the power.

If there are more seats held by the opposition, then it is said that the country has a minority government. In such instances, which are rare in Canada, the ruling party must satisfy the opposition or it will be brought down by a vote of no confidence. In such a scenario, the House will be dissolved and a new election will be called. Generally speaking, minority governments last only a few months at best, but the Conservative Party under Stephen Harper managed to survive as a minority government from 2006 to 2011.

The House of Commons is divided into two sides, with rows of padded benches facing each other across a central floor.   At the head of the House, on a magnificently carved wood throne sits the Speaker of the House. He or she is elected by the members, and serves to guide the debates. The Speaker is a very important individual as he or she can limit debate, order the Sergeant at Arms to eject members who are unruly and in general is the guiding force behind the debates. Only in the event of a tie does the Speaker cast a vote. The party in power sits on the benches to the Speaker's right, with the Prime Minister and cabinet ministers occupying the center of the front bench. To the left of the Speaker sit the members of the opposition, arranged by the number of seats held by each opposition party. The Leader of the Opposition sits in the center of the front bench opposite the Prime Minister.

Only the party in power may generally introduce new legislation. Once a bill has been introduced, it is debated in a mixture of English and French since every member is expected to be linguistically competent in both languages. Perhaps changes will be required to satisfy objections from the opposition, or even to appease members within the ruling party itself. After various changes, further readings and debates, the question is called. Members then vote on the bill and if it receives a majority of votes, it is then sent on to the Senate for their recommendation to the Governor General. If there are no Senate objections, the bill is passed to the Governor General for Royal Assent to enable it to become law. If the ruling party cannot get a bill passed, it is then up to the opposition to call for a vote of confidence. This simply means that the entire house votes as to its confidence in the party in power to continue to rule. A vote of no confidence then causes the House of Commons to be dissolved and a national election to be called. No confidence votes are rare in Canada as there have been few occasions when a minority government sits on the Speaker's right. As long as the ruling party maintains a comfortable majority, it is virtually impossible for the opposition to bring them down. Only if dissident members of the ruling party, those considered by party leadership to be mavericks, decide to vote with the opposition is it possible to secure a non-confidence vote.

There is a great flexibility to the Canadian Parliament. The House of Commons is truly subject to the power of debate. So long as the people choose one party and give it a sizeable majority, there is stability in the ability of that party to govern. If the people are not set on the ability of one party and vote in such a manner as to elect a minority government, then they are literally forced to choose again as such a minority leadership is sure to bring about a vote of no confidence. If the party in power should face a major scandal, a non-confidence vote is sure to occur, as even party members will want to return to the voters to revalidate their claim to power. Often within the party itself, the leadership can be changed if there is either scandal or a lack of internal confidence in the head of the party. Thus the country can see a new Prime Minister without the need for an election. This happened in 1991 when after introducing what became the hated Goods and Services Tax, Prime Minister Brian Mulroney stepped down due to internal party pressure. Kim Campbell became the newly appointed Conservative leader. After only three months in office, she decided to call for a public election to see if the Conservatives could strengthen their lead. It was a risky move, but she was so confident in her personal appeal that she went ahead with the election. As a result of this hated federal tax on all goods and services except vitals such as food, the public punished the Conservatives by sweeping them from a comfortable majority to only remaining with two seats in the House of Commons. They were essentially obliterated politically. It took them until 2006 to regain strength and only as a minority government.

Politics in Canada can often be quite unpredictable, and the May 3, 2011 election proved to be quite an upset in several quarters. The Conservative Party led by Stephen Harper won a substantial majority of 166 seats, making it impossible for a vote of no confidence to occur. Thus the Conservative Party had a full five-year mandate from the people to follow through on its agenda. But Steven Harper asked for the dissolving of Parliament in late summer 2015, thinking he could possibly strengthen his position. All of the polls predicted that at best the Conservative Party would hold on to its majority, or even possibly come back as a minority government. There was also some hope in many circles that the New Democratic Party could form a minority government. And the news media and pollsters were saying that the Liberal Party under the young leader Justin Trudeau would come in third and even possibly loose a few of its seats. Nobody seemed to recognize the young leader's charm, charismatic personality and appeal. Not only did the party win, but also it came in with a strong majority. Now the 44-year-old Right Honourable Prime Minister Justin Trudeau is the talk of the nation and around the world. He is exceptionally good looking, charming and brings the country full circle back to the days when his late father swept the nation in 1968. To date the Liberal Party has survived two elections with Trudeau as Prime Minister, but as a minority party. With support from the New Democratic Party their power is assured until the next election in 2025.

The annual session of Parliament is opened with pomp and ceremony each fall. The Governor General rides from his or her residence at Rideau Hall in an open carriage along with a mounted honor guard of Royal Canadian Mounted Police to Parliament Hill. Inside the Senate Chamber, sitting on a gold throne, The Governor General calls for the members of the House of Commons to be summoned. In a tradition that harkens back to Britain during the days when the monarch's soldiers could invade the House of Commons, the doors to the Commons are barred. The Senate's representative, known as the Gentleman Usher of the Black Rod, must knock three times to be admitted. Then in the name of the Crown he summons the members to attend the Governor General at the bar (entrance) of the Senate Chamber. Only the Prime Minister and Leader of the Opposition are permitted inside the Chamber while the rest of the Commons must crowd together at the railing just inside of the entrance. The Governor General then reads the Speech from the Throne, which outlines what the House of Commons, expects to accomplish during the upcoming session. In actuality, the Prime Minister and the Cabinet write the speech. On those occasions when Her Majesty The Queen has visited Canada in the fall, she then has the duty of opening Parliament. But given the current age of Her Majesty it is doubtful she will journey to Canada herself in the future/

The House of Commons chamber (currently under extensive renovation). (Work of Jeangagnon, CC BY SA 4.0, Wikimedia.org)

The provincial governments function in the same manner as the federal government. Each province has a Lieutenant Governor who is the queen's representative. There is a provincial legislature that follows the same basic principles of governance as the federal parliament. Only in Québec it is named the National Assembly, this an outgrowth of the years of separatist influence from the late 1960's to the early 1990's when there was a strong faction that wanted to have the province become an independent nation.

* CANADA'S JUDICIARY: The court system of Canada is based upon the principle that the judiciary serves the Crown. Judges at all levels are appointed, never elected as in the United States. The courts are layered from the highest appeals court down to local municipal courts, but all judges serve as agents of the Crown.

* The Supreme Court of Canada: Consisting of nine justices, three of who must always be from Québec, this august body is the highest appeals court in the nation. It hears appeals from the provincial courts in both civil and criminal matters. The Court is located in Ottawa.

* The Exchequer Court: This court, which also sits in Ottawa, deals with revenue matters and claims against the Crown. The Exchequer Court also deals with all matters concerning navigable rivers and ports with regard to navigation and shipping.

* Provincial Superior Courts: Depending upon the size of the province, there may be various branches to the provincial superior court system. Each province has a Court of Appeals and a trial court, known as either the High Court or the Court of Queen's Bench.

* Provincial Inferior Courts: These are the lower courts of each province and include such matters as probate, family, juvenile, small debt and local municipal courts.

* **POLICE IN CANADA:** All police in Canada serve as agents of the Crown. There is no secret police of any sort.

A proud Royal Canadian Mounted Police constable, (Work of Mark Kortum, CC BY SA 2.0, Wikimedia.org)

* Royal Canadian Mounted Police: This highly respected force, which dates back to the frontier days of the Prairies, is the national police of Canada. They serve to uphold the law in all provinces and local jurisdictions that have not organized their own police forces. In addition, they provide security for federal buildings and key governmental personnel. The traditional red coat uniform is only worn for

ceremonial purposes. In addition to policing, the RCMP also maintains crime labs and performs investigative services as well as liaison with foreign criminal justice agencies.

The Royal Canadian Mounted Police badge

* **Provincial Police:** Only Ontario, Québec and Newfoundland maintain a provincial force to police rural areas and those municipalities that do not have their own municipal police departments.

The Sûreté du Québec in a winter parade (Work of Asclepias, CC BY SA 3.0, Wikimedia.org)

* **Municipal Police:** Most Canadian cities maintain their own municipal police departments to provide services within their corporate limits.

* CANADA'S MILITARY: Canada maintains a unified military known as the Canadian Defence Force. It is comprised of three branches; army, navy and air force. Each service maintains its own distinct traditions, uniforms and rank structure. The primary role of the military is to protect the nation, but Canadian forces have served in many foreign campaigns. As a part of the British Commonwealth of Nations, Canadian troops served with distinction in the Boer War, World War I and World War II. As a member of the United Nations, Canadian forces have served on peacekeeping missions in numerous countries, always garnering great respect as Canada is looked upon as a major world power despite its small population. As a member of the North Atlantic Treaty Organization, Canadian forces participated in peacekeeping missions in the former Yugoslavia. And as an important ally of the United States, Canada provided forces in both the first and second Persian Gulf Wars. And in fall 2014, the Canadian government authorized six jet fighters to participate in the coalition fighting ISIS in Iraq and Syria, but the new Liberal government brought them back.

Today Canada is providing on the ground technical and advisory support to the government of Iraq. And in 2022 the government has shown strong support for Ukraine in its war with Russia. The Prime Minister has gone on record with condemnation of Russia's brutal military actions. The province of Manitoba is today home to the largest population of Ukrainians of any place in the world outside of the Ukraine itself.

We may be a melting pot of people from many nations, but our spirit as a nation is especially strong. We are all Canadians.

THE DISTINCTIVE CANADIAN CULTURE

When American visitors say, "Canada is just like the United States," I literally see red with anger. We share the same high standard of living and many of the material aspects of culture with the United States, but those are only superficial in nature. But below the surface are so many vast differences, and many of these do manifest themselves visually in the landscape. And in Québec with its very strong French traditions and language, you would never for a minute think you were anywhere south of the border. Overall you will find more differences than you will similarities. And soon you will recognize that you are in a different country. It is so important to understand the basic characteristics of Canadian and Québécois cultures and everyday life so as to appreciate the country when visiting its major cities or rural areas. So I repeat, those who say that Canada is just like the United States are absolutely wrong. Even the perceived visual similarities are superficial, as there is a decidedly Canadian architecture. But on the whole the sight of gasoline stations, strip malls, large shopping malls, housing tracts and other such facets do create a degree of similarity until one looks deeper.

The overall standard of living in Canada and the United States are on the whole similar. But the big difference lies in the fact that approximately 90 percent of Canadian families would be placed in the broad middle class category. There are percentage wise relatively few extremely poor Canadians and urban slums like those found in many large American cities are essentially absent. Likewise there is only a small segment of the population that would be classified as extremely wealthy. Canada has more middle ground as a nation with regard to wealth distribution, and this has a great positive impact upon the overall daily life of the people.

CANADIAN CITIES: Unlike their American counterparts, Canadian cities are exceptionally clean, very vibrant and relatively crime free. Urban blight and decay are not the ongoing problem that most American urban centers must contend with. The question raised is why? Essentially Canadian cities owe their greater economic success, a large middle class, strong government, a good social welfare net and a level of pride that is innate to the culture itself. Here are a few distinct visual observations of urban life:

* Downtown: The downtown core of Canadian cities is the center of economic and social life. Flight to the suburbs does not have to mean an abandonment of the inner city, and Canada is proof of that fact. However, whereas young families move to the suburbs, working singles and many executives choose to live in and around the downtown core, thus breathing great life into the city's hub. The downtown of any Canadian city is a mix of high-rise office buildings, major hotels, large department

stores, theatres, concert halls, restaurants and museums. It is the place to go for retail services and entertainment. But above all, it is the focus of high-rise apartment or condominium living with rents or sales prices maintained at high levels due to demand. There is also the factor of fast and efficient public transportation. The major cities of Montréal, Toronto, Vancouver, Ottawa, Edmonton and Calgary all possess a subway, light rail and/or commuter train service into the downtown core. In all other cities, busses and electric trolleys are to be found.

Stephen's Walk is the heart of pedestrian shopping in downtown Calgary.

* Neighborhood Shopping: Canadian cities are very much like those of Europe in that each residential neighborhood has its own shopping district, providing a myriad of small grocers, delicatessens, bakeries and produce markets, often with distinct ethnic flavors. In addition, neighborhood-shopping districts offer all basic services plus the ever-present florist and garden shops. Canadians consider fresh flowers and home gardening as two distinct passions.

* Dining Out: Restaurants abound in Canadian cities. There is a strong interest in dining out, both in the city core and in local neighborhoods. Many of the restaurants are of the specialty or ethnic variety. Meals in Canadian restaurants are served with a distinct Old World flair. Tablecloths are the norm rather than the exception in most restaurants. Menus are extensive and offer great varieties in seafood, richly prepared dishes containing sauces, fresh vegetables and elegant breads. Dessert is another Canadian passion. It is rare to see diners pass on dessert, and the offerings are in keeping with European tradition – pastries, tortes

and cakes of the most incredible flavors and textures. And this tradition is strongest in the province of Québec, as it would be in France.

High-rise apartments and condominiums dominate so much of Toronto

The main shopping street of Trois Rivières, Québec, a city of 100,000

* Housing: Single-family homes are similar to those in adjacent regions of the United States, with some minor variation. In eastern Canada, brick and wood are predominant building materials while in the Prairie Provinces and British Columbia; most houses utilize thick, unpainted stucco faced with wood trim. High-rise apartments and condominiums are a very dominant part of Canadian urban centers from small towns to the largest cities. Canada seems to be literally infatuated with high-rise living. All major downtown areas are honeycombed and surrounded by vast numbers of modern residential towers while the outer city regions show clusters of apartments and condominiums, thus presenting an impressive skyline that extends from one end of the city to the other. Most apartments and condominiums have large balconies, sometimes glassed in to serve as a winter solarium. Toronto, Canada's largest city has more high-rise buildings than any other city in North America. Vancouver, with a metropolitan population of just over 2 million, has more high-rise buildings than Chicago with five times its population. Halifax with only 500,000 in its metro area is experiencing quite a significant boom in the construction of high-rise apartments in the city center and the suburbs. But Montréal does have a greater percentage of row houses or semi-detached housing than what is found in Toronto. Both single-family houses and high-rise buildings are generally landscaped with impeccable detail. Most Canadians have a great love for gardening during their brief summers. The majority of Canadian households possess hardwood floors rather than carpeting. Otherwise the amenities are the same as in the United States.

* Parks and Gardens: Canadian cities devote vast acreage to public parks and gardens, especially along waterways or lakefronts. On a per capita basis, Canadians have more than four times the acreage of parks than Americans. With low crime rates, people are able to make good use of public parks. In many cities, there are systems of walking trails that often interconnect parklands with each other and the surrounding neighborhoods. During the spring and summer months, the plantings of various floral displays enhance the visual appearance of parks, making them prime locations for photographing bridal parties. At Montréal's Botanical Garden, Vancouver's Queen Elizabeth Park and Toronto's Edwards Gardens, bridal groups reserve ahead so as to be able to have their portraits taken amid enormous floral gardens.

* Public Buildings: Most governmental buildings are designed in a British or French Gothic style, usually constructed of stone and capped with pitched copper roofs that oxidize into a distinct turquoise or greenish color. Ottawa possesses the greatest array of such monumental buildings, as it is the national capital. Each provincial capital has numerous buildings that house the provincial legislatures and governmental offices. Museums and university buildings also exhibit this distinctly European style, as do many of the older railway stations.

TRANSPORTATION SERVICES: Canada has an extensive system of highways that span all populated portions of the country. The Trans-Canada

Highway is the longest identified route in the world, extending from St. John's, Newfoundland to Victoria, British Columbia, a distance in excess of 8,050 kilometers or 5,000 miles, and including two ferryboat connections. Each province has its own system of road numbering apart from the national TC-1 Highway. And in Québec it has been mandated by provincial law that all highway signs are written in French only, which can be a bit intimidating for English speaking visitors.

There are two railroads operating in the country – Canadian National and Canadian Pacific, often providing parallel service. A Crown Corporation known as Via Rail Canada now provides all passenger service. Unlike the American Amtrak, Via Rail provides outstanding service and is well patronized. Trains are modern, exceptionally clean and offer both standard and Via One (first class) services. On the transcontinental train known as "The Canadian" and on the east coast connection known as the "Ocean," first class sleeping car service is available. Sleeping car service is also offered between Jasper National Park, Alberta and Prince Rupert, British Columbia.

Air service is offered throughout the nation by Air Canada with feeder lines serving more remote locations. Air Canada also offers international service and is ranked by travel sources as being among the world's best airlines. There are a few small, regional carriers and charter services, but Air Canada is the primary carrier for the nation. There are now a few budget carriers, but they are no match for Air Canada in their scope of service with the exception of WestJet.

CANADIAN TRADITIONS: There are many distinctly Canadian customs entering into everyday life that illustrate the Canadian distinctiveness.

* Canadians consider the drinking of tea to be a significant symbol of their British, French and general European heritage. Coffee is widely consumed, but tea is still the primary beverage, and is served in most restaurants boiling hot and already brewed. Also tea is normally seen ahead of coffee when looking at the order of beverages on a restaurant menu.

* In the service of a meal, most Canadians still set their tables with a greater degree of Old World flair than Americans. Most households consider a set of fine china to be an essential element. Department stores and specialty china shops offer a great selection in a variety of price ranges so that most households can afford it.

* Sweetshops, tea and coffee houses and refreshment stands abound in all Canadian cities and towns, both downtown and in neighborhood shopping areas. And in Québec this tradition reaches its zenith. Québécois pastries are the best in the nation.

A typical pastry counter in Vancouver

* The use of outdoor decorations of gourds and Indian corn to usher in the coming of the fall season is a widespread tradition across the country, especially for Canadian Thanksgiving held on the second Monday of October. And Halloween is a big holiday with many Canadians decorating the exterior of their homes in quite an elaborate manner.

* At a more traditional dinner party, dessert is often no served at the same sitting as the meal. Guests adjourn into the living room for conversation while the hostess clears the table, and then resets it with fresh service before putting out a variety of fruits and desserts, generally to be served around two hours after the conclusion of the meal. But this custom is dying out among younger families

* Canadians consider it patriotic to display the national maple leaf emblem on backpacks, sweatshirts, briefcases or other personal items. Depicting the maple leaf and the national colors of red and white on billboards, holiday decorations or other displays is not viewed as a desecration of the country's symbol. And in Québec, the provincial flag is equally well displayed. For many years, most Québécois would only fly the provincial flag, but today the national flag is more widely seen. However, the National Assembly, which is the provincial parliament, still only flies the Québec flag.

CANADIAN HOLIDAYS: Like the United States, Canada celebrates New Year's Day, Labour Day (notice the Canadian spelling) and Christmas as public holidays. In addition, there are many holidays apart from those recognized in the United States. Queen Victoria's birthday, known as Victoria Day is celebrated on the third Monday of May. The Province of Québec has its own holiday known as Fête de la St-Jean Baptiste, held on the 24th of June. The people of Québec have made it one and the same with their separatist movement. Thanksgiving is celebrated on the second Monday of October, and it is a festival of the harvest and has nothing to do with the Pilgrims. The entire weekend is devoted to dining and/or enjoying the autumn colors in the countryside. Remembrance Day is a time for honoring war heroes and veterans, and it is the same day that Americans call Veteran's Day – November 11th. The wearing of red paper poppies is still a strong part of Remembrance Day. On the day following Christmas, Canada celebrates Boxing Day, a tradition that goes back to Britain and is honored in most commonwealth nations.

SPORTING EVENTS: Canada is synonymous with hockey. It is the country's claim to fame, but to Canadians it is a national event. Little children can be seen with their hockey sticks walking to the nearest ice rink or frozen pond from as young as age five. On Monday night the majority of Canadians tune in to CBC television for a televised game on what is called "Hockey Night in Canada." In addition to hockey, Canadians also take an interest in lacrosse, a game originally played by the Native American tribes of eastern Canada. During winter, curling is another popular game and curling rinks can be found all across the country.

Canadian football is based upon the American game, but with a variety of minor differences such as the field consisting of 110 yards, this despite the fact that Canada has officially been on the metric system since the early 1970's. Baseball and basketball are gaining in popularity, but there is only one major league baseball and basketball team in the nation, both in Toronto. Outdoor activities such as fishing, hiking and hunting are popular among both urban and rural residents. As a show of the popularity of the great outdoors, it is important to note the development of the Trans-Canada Trail. A private non-profit organization has sponsored donations for the construction of a series of interconnected hiking trails that span the nation from the Atlantic to the Pacific, with a branch to the Arctic shore. When completed, this will be the largest such trail system in the world. All along its length, there are pavilions in which plaques honor contributors, with many names being inscribed in memory of departed loved ones.

THE CANADIAN LANGUAGES: Fortunately for Americans, the use of the English language in Canada is not that different from that of the United States. Unlike Australian English, the Canadian version has only a few minor variations from the American version. There are some differences in both vocabulary and pronunciation. The most common give away that somebody is Canadian is by his or her use of the term, "eh?" either as a statement of emphasis or as a question. For example, a Canadian might say, "Nice day today, eh?" Also there is a measure of distinctness to such words as "out" and "again" that has a slight hint of the British intonation. With regard to vocabulary, a few very Canadian terms are' broadlooms, Chesterfield, garburetor, Loonie, Riding, serviette and Twoonie. In American English these terms mean; wall-to-wall carpeting, sofa, garbage disposal, one-dollar coin, parliamentary election district, napkin and two dollar coin. And these are just a few examples.

Then there is the matter of spelling. Canada uses the British format in spelling, which can be frustrating for Americans. A few examples are; colour, defence, favourite, harbour and plateaux all showing both British and French influences.

The French dialect spoken in Québec and by French-Canadians across the nation differs significantly from the French spoken in France. Essentially, Canadian French is rooted in the colonial heritage and has many expressions not found in France. In addition, pronunciations differ from those of France. It is referred to as Québécois rather than French among francophone (those who speak French). In most rural parts of Québec you will find older people who do not speak English since they grow up in a francophone environment and remain tied to their local community. Today, in the schools English is taught as the second language so that the young Québécois are bilingual, but choose to speak French most of the time.

THE USE OF THE METRIC SYSTEM: Canada joined the majority of nations of the world by converting to the metric system in 1973. Thus in Canada, distances are measured in meters and kilometers, liquids are measured in liters and solid weight in kilograms. When watching a weather forecast, temperatures are given in degrees Celsius and wind speed in kilometers while barometric pressure is shown in kilopascals. But when buying real estate or floor coverings, units are still quoted in square feet. Nobody knows why.

THE CANADIAN MEDIA: Canada has an active publishing industry. Canadian authors in both English and French have a wide audience, and bookstores devote much of their shelf space to Canadian literature. The federal government regulates the magazine publishing industry in that foreign publishers that wish to produce a Canadian edition must devote 50 percent of the content to Canadian topics as well as featuring Canadian advertising. This has limited the expansion of American publications into Canada for the sake of adding to their advertising revenue by issuing so called Canadian editions that were nothing more than the American content with Canadian advertising. Newspapers are found in all parts of the country, either in English or French, but the most widely read newspaper is the "Globe and Mail," published in several regional editions.

Radio and television show a distinct competitive trend in that the federal government and private broadcasters vie with each other for market share. The Canadian Broadcasting Corporation, better known as the CBC is a Crown Corporation, heavily funded by the federal government. It produces outstanding programming and also is known for its Monday night hockey and its superb evening news program, "The National." The Canadian Television Network or CTV is second in scope to the CBC. There are numerous local and cable stations now offering greater variety. Throughout the country, English and French radio and television will be found, but in Québec, French stations totally outnumber those broadcasting in English. All radio and television network stations are identified by call letters that begin with "C."

CURRENCY: Canada maintains one of the world's most colorful sets of currency. Approximately every ten years, the government reissues its bank notes utilizing totally new designs. Despite these design changes, the color combinations always remain the same.

The current issue of Canadian banknotes

Canada no longer uses a dollar or two-dollar note, but has opted for a brass dollar coin featuring the image of a loon on the obverse side, thus its nickname as the "loonie." The two-dollar coin has a brass interior, surrounded by an aluminized outer ring and features a polar bear on the obverse. It has been dubbed the "twoonie." It may sound like baby talk to an outsider, but we think nothing of referring to loonies and twoonies.

Paper denominations include a blue five-dollar note, a purple ten-dollar note, a light green twenty-dollar note, an orange fifty-dollar note and a brown hundred-dollar note. Small coins include copper one-cent, aluminized coins in five, ten and twenty-five cent denominations; all are similar in size to those of the United States. A portrait of Queen Elizabeth appears on all coins, and she appears on the twenty-dollar bank note. Other bank notes feature portraits of famous Canadian prime ministers. The present series of banknotes is printed on a polymer material rather than paper and is far more durable and harder to counterfeit.

The new 2018 vertical ten-dollar note picturing Viola Desmond, a Nova Scotia woman of color who defied a movie theater's segregated seating in 1946. Today her courage is honored by the nation

The one dollar coin known as the "Loonie"

THE GEOGRAPHIC CHARACTER OF THE NATIONAL CAPITAL REGION

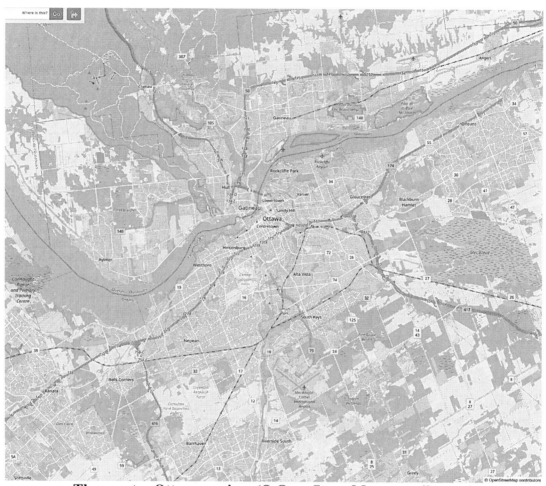

The greater Ottawa region, (© OpenStreetMap contributors)

OTTAWA GEOGRAPHY: The city of Ottawa is located along the southern bank of the great Ottawa River, which flows out of the interior Canadian Shield and flows to the southeast to where it joins the St. Lawrence River. The Ottawa River forms a good portion of the lower border between the provinces of Ontario and Québec. The urban area of greater Ottawa is an interprovincial region often referred to as the Outaouais by the Québécois, but that term should properly just refer to the Québec side of the river. Officially the term National Capital Region is what should be used in reference to the entire urban area. Nowhere else in Canada is there a major urban region straddling a provincial border.

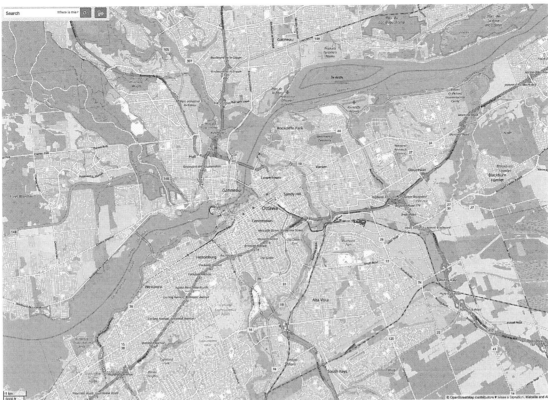

The basic layout of the Ottawa urban area, (© OpenStreetMap contributors)

The core of Ottawa and Gatineau, (© OpenStreetMap contributors)

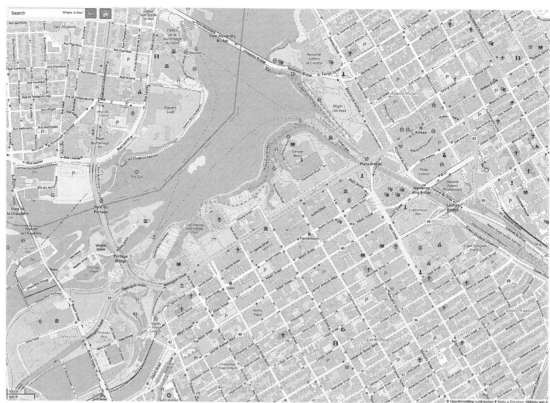

The Parliament Hill area, (© OpenStreetMap contributors

Looking down upon Parliament Hill, (Work of tsaiproject, CC BY SA 2.0, Wikimedia.org)

On the Ontario side of the Ottawa River the land is gently rolling and is primarily devoted to farming. There are small patches of the original deciduous forest cover, especially along rivers, streams and around the numerous lakes that dot the landscape. It is quite beautiful in a more idyllic and manicured fashion similar to that of the English countryside. There are numerous back roads, small villages and towns giving the landscape an intricate pattern of developed use combined with many natural reserves where the beauty is still preserved.

The Ottawa suburbs merge with lush farmland, (Work of Joyce Lundrigan, CC BY SA 3.0, Wikimedia.org)

On the Québec side of the Ottawa River there is only a narrow fringe of level ground that is partly suburban and the remainder devoted to farmland similar to the Ontario side, but architecturally the French flavor is quite noticeable and it is easy to know you are in Québec and not in Ontario.

The Gatineau Hills rise relatively quickly out of the farmland, giving the northern shore more of a rugged appearance, as some elevations are as high as 1,000 meters or 3,300 feet. Much of the landscape immediately north and west of the Québec suburb of Hull is preserved as the vast and beautiful Gatineau National Park. The park occupies 361 square kilometers or 139 square miles. It contains numerous small lakes, thick deciduous forests and many panoramic vistas. There are also several villages that dot the landscape, giving it a different visual flavor than the more gentle lands on the Ontario side of the Ottawa River. Summer and fall tourism are especially important to the Gatineau Hills.

Fall along the escarpment in Gatineau National Park, (Work of cjuneau, CC BY SA 2.0, Wikimedia.org)

Agriculture in the entire National Capital Region consists of dairy farming, vegetable gardens and orchards. There is very little large scale corporate farming with most of the land held by families. This region is quite productive and supplies both metropolitan Ottawa and Montréal with produce and dairy products.

The seasonal march throughout the greater Ottawa region is quite pronounced. Spring begins in mid-April on most years. In Ottawa it is celebrated with the planting of millions of tulip bulbs, more to be said later in the book. Fruit orchards and local plantings give forth a riot of blooms. As the snow begins to melt, the sap runs up in the thousands of maple trees, and the sugaring season is a major event. This region considers its maple syrup as a significant commodity and source of pride.

Summer in the region is warm with occasional days where temperatures can soar into the mid 30's Celsius or upper 80's Fahrenheit. Rainfall is quite regularly distributed during summer. Tornadoes or massive thunderstorms are occasionally seen, but are not a significant worry.

The most celebrated season is fall. The greater Ottawa region is noted for its brilliant autumn leaves. This is a season for heavy tourist activity, as the local cultures, history and colors combine to make this a memorable time for visitors. As a Canadian with my roots in both Ontario and Québec, I personally treat the fall color season as an almost religious experience, as do many millions of residents and visitors alike.

A fall farmer's market tent near Perth, west of Ottawa

Early winter in the Gatineau before the heavy snowfall

Winter throughout the greater Ottawa region is long and quite cold. Snowfall can accumulate to significant amounts, again giving the landscape a very picturesque appearance. There is limited winter sport activity, as the higher Laurentian Mountains to the north, closer to Montréal is a major winter sports playground.

The depth of a Québec winter, (Work of Claude Brochu, C BY SA 3.0, Wikimedia.org)

OTTAWA AS THE NATION'S CAPITAL

As the national capital of Canada the city of Ottawa has no rival. It is not possible to compare the overall flavor of Ottawa with any other city in Canada since it has no equal. In addition to being the federal capital, it is the center of a major metropolitan area that spreads over the landscape of two provinces. With the lifestyles of Ontario and Québec being so diametrically opposite, the bringing together of these two distinct cultures in one metropolitan region is in itself unique. In many ways, Ottawa expresses the ideal profile of Canada – a nation that is officially bilingual and bicultural. No other urban environment meets that definition better than Ottawa. To best appreciate the city of Ottawa, it is important to trace its evolution and growth because had it not been chosen as the national capital it is doubtful that it would even exist as a city.

Early explorers who sailed up the St. Lawrence River and who entered the Ottawa River found that the rapids made continuous navigation difficult, if not next to impossible. They were exploring less for settlement than they were in trying to find a route through this new and massive landmass, looking for a passage through to the Pacific Ocean and on to China.

The first feeble attempts at settlement were made by missionaries in the very early 1600's, but they had little success. It was not until 1800 when a small group of families led by Philemon Wright from New England attempted to establish a small agricultural community in what is today Hull, Québec. They found that it was more lucrative to exploit timber than it was to farm because of the severity of the winter. The cut wood could be piled on the ice of the frozen river and then in spring it would be rafted down the Ottawa River and then the St. Lawrence River to where there was a small market in Montréal and Ville de Québec (Québec City).

Settlement in what is today Ottawa began in 1826 when word was out that a canal was being engineered by the British Military to connect their fortress at Kingston on Lake Ontario with their forces in Montréal and Ville de Québec. This would avoid the close proximity to American forces along what is now the New York border of the St. Lawrence River, as relations between the United State and Britain after the War of 1812 were still tenuous. The initial town became known as Bytown, a name still carried by this original portion of Ottawa just to the east of Parliament Hill that surrounds the Byward Market. The completion of the canal provided a safe link between the settled core of Ontario around Toronto and Montréal long before the development of railroads. This link encouraged settlers to begin to develop the Ottawa River Valley around Bytown.

The Canal followed the natural contour of the land and bifurcated the newly developed town into the flats overlooking the river that became known as Lower Town and the Upper Town where ultimately the parliament buildings would be constructed. Today Lower Town is what everyone locally calls Bytown and Upper Town ultimately developed into Parliament Hill and downtown Ottawa.

When Bytown incorporated, the name Ottawa was chosen, coming from the Algonquin language and meaning a place where trade occurs. It was an appropriate name. In 1857 Queen Victoria was asked to select a location for the capital of the united Province of Canada after the union of the colonies of Upper Canada (Ontario) and Lower Canada (Québec) in 1841. The logic behind the choice, which most are sure her advisors recommended, was its somewhat isolated position, surrounded by forest and less exposed to potential American attack. And geographically it was well situated between Kingston, Ontario and Ville de Québec. As the capital of the newly united colony, it was a meeting place for both trade and government. In today's reality it is closer to Montréal than to Toronto. Culturally it is strongly influenced by the Québécois culture a fact that worried many people with strong English ties.

In the present day there is a certain degree of discomfort among government bodies in that the city of Ottawa looks to Toronto with regard to provincial matters in such aspects as funding since the seat of provincial government is at Queen's Park in Toronto. Yet at the same the city of Ottawa is the host to the federal government. Unlike the United States and Australia a federal jurisdiction such as the District of Columbia or the Australian Capital Territory was not created. And being that many government offices are located across the river from Parliament Hill in Hull-Gatineau, the federal government must work closely with provincial authorities in both Ontario and Québec.

Ottawa grew rapidly after it was chosen to be the colonial capital city, especially after 1867 when Canada became the first independent nation within the British Empire, thus the oldest member nation of the Commonwealth apart from the United Kingdom. But apart from a few prominent and government buildings, Ottawa and Hull were primarily built of wood and had a frontier flavor.

With an abundance of timber in the surrounding countryside many early eastern Canadian cities were built mainly out of wood, and like other communities the Ottawa area suffered a significant fire in 1900, destroying much of Hull and then was spread by embers carried on the wind into central Ottawa, causing an equal amount of destruction. As the area recovered, the use of brick and stone replaced wood as the principal building material for even single family homes. Today Ottawa is a city of brown stone and red brick, as are Toronto and Montréal.

A rooftop view of the Ottawa-Hull fire of 1900

Construction of the colonial parliament buildings began in 1859 with granite chosen as the primary building material. And the style was more of a neo gothic, mirroring that seen in London and Paris. The buildings were still under construction when the four major colonies of Ontario, Québec, New Brunswick and Nova Scotia joined in Confederation in 1867 as the first Dominion that would become the foundation for the British Commonwealth of Nations. A more localized fire in 1916 heavily damaged the Centre Block, but it was able to be saved and restored. Restoration was completed by 1922 and the Peace Tower, which dominates over Parliament Hill was added.

The small triangular piece of land to the east of the parliament buildings became the site for the National War Memorial in 1939, which today is considered to be the heart of Ottawa. It is here that major memorial services are held each year on November 11, known in Canada and Remembrance Day.

By 1890, Ottawa had electric street lights, electric street lights and also showed off its first parks that surrounded the buildings on Parliament Hill.

By the time the Parliament building was constructed, the land across the river in Hull, Québec became the site for one of the world's largest lumber mills. Looking across from the windows in the parliament buildings the view was one of industrial blight that stood in sharp contrast to the grounds upon which the government stood. It formed a blight on the landscape until the mid-20th century when it was replaced by many government ministries that today compliment Parliament Hill. In 1950, a master plan was established to oversee the development of parklands, the landscaping of government buildings and an orderly beautification of the city to showcase its importance as the national capital.

What would become the site of the National War Memorial as it appeared at the end of the 19th century

The Centre Block of Parliament in 1901

Today urban beautification is a very serious business and Ottawa is one of the most carefully landscaped cities in all of Canada. The banks of the Rideau Canal are set aside as a parkland that cuts across the core of the city. And thanks to an annual gift from the government of the Netherlands, a million tulip bulbs are planted each year on Crown lands in the city. During World War II, Ottawa gave sanctuary to the crown princess of the Netherlands and today a tulip festival is held each spring. This is an event that draws both locals and visitors out to appreciate the myriad beds of blooms that brighten Ottawa after the long winter.

The lumber mills that faced Parliament Hill until the end of the 1950's

Apart from its role as the seat of government, Ottawa came of age as an important manufacturing center when high tech companies chose to locate here, bringing the metropolitan population by 2022 to 1,423,000, making it the fourth largest city in Canada just edging out Calgary by a few thousand residents. But because the metropolitan area is split between the provinces of Ontario and Québec, Calgary can still claim itself to be the fourth largest. This is of course a matter of definition, but also a source of urban pride. Ottawa is often spoken of in the high tech communities of the world as "Canada's Silicon Valley."

As the federal capital, many important visitors come each year for diplomatic conferences or formal visits. And being the center of power it also attracts tourists who come to visit its museums, galleries and to explore the various monuments to the nation's pride.

As Ottawa grew on the Ontario side of the river, many of the former small satellite communities have been absorbed into the Ottawa-Carlton Metropolitan Area while the suburbs on the Québec side have become the city of Gatineau. These amalgamations ultimately provide for better governmental services and eliminate much of the duplication of effort by smaller communities.

The view across the Ottawa River from Parliament Hill today

Transportation still is divided in that there are only a handful of bus lines that interconnect the Ontario and Québec communities. However, a new light rail system is in its earliest stages of development in Ontario. If it meets expectations it could ultimately become a unified service for both Ontario and Québec residents in the greater Ottawa community. The issue of the metropolitan area being split between two provinces is complicated by the linguistic history of Canada. This is the only heavily populated area in the nation that is split between primarily English speaking Ontario and French speaking Québec. And both sides hold their languages to be almost sacrosanct. For example, when I visit Ottawa, I stay at either the Westin or Andaz Hotels and also avail myself of a rental car. The only gas station that is easily accessible to these two major hotels is an Esso station just across the Alexandra Bridge in Hull. But in order to get any services at that station it is imperative to be able to speak to the staff in French. Fortunately for me it is no problem. But for many this poses a problem and is an illustration of the little nuances of touring around metropolitan Ottawa.

But despite some visitors having bit of a language issue, they will find that people in greater Ottawa are welcoming and visitors are treated with courtesy. It is after all the Canadian Way!

ARRIVING IN THE CITY

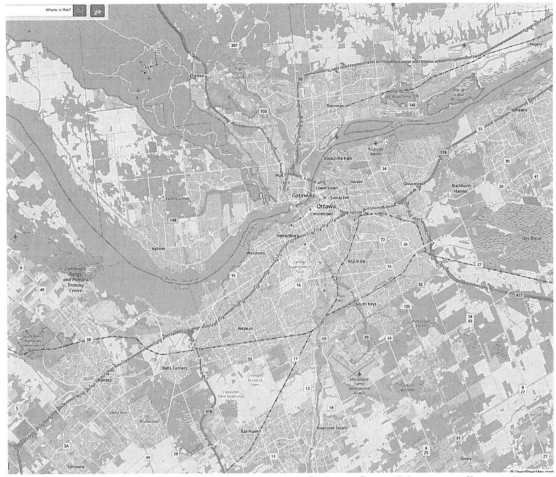

The Ottawa express highway network, (© OpenStreetMap contributors)

By the time you reach this chapter of the book, I hope you are considering a visit to Ottawa and are ready to plan your trip. Many of you who are reading this will no doubt be visiting Ottawa during the spring or summer when the roads are free of snow or ice and the temperatures are especially pleasant. Although there is a fair segment of readers who enjoy coming during winter, as the national capital takes on a very distinct flavor when covered in snow. There is also local skiing just outside of the immediate urban area. But the best skiing is found in the Laurentian Mountains at Mont Tremblant, which is only 153 kilometers or 95 miles away, a driving time of just under two hours.

To begin your visit to Ottawa we need to look at how do you arrive. There are some important facts to consider:

* **Do you need a passport? If you are living outside of Canada the answer is yes! All visitors to Canada, including expatriate Canadians and Americans need to have a valid passport. Other than visitors from the United States, United Kingdom and the**

European Union countries, the remainder of visitors may need a visitor's visa. It is best to check with the Canadian consulate to be sure. A new law went into effect in late 2016 that applies to dual Canadian citizens except if their other country of citizenship is the United States. All Canadians who hold a second passport from another country (other than the United States) where they live or work now must have a valid Canadian passport to enter the country.

* If you are driving a car from the United States into Canada all you need to have is a valid registration and an interprovincial insurance card issued by your American auto insurance company. Ottawa is 98.8 kilometers or 61.3 miles from the main border crossing at Prescott, Ontario and Ogdensburg, New York, crossing the St. Lawrence River between the two ports of entry. However, Ogdensburg is a fair distance from the main population centers of the eastern United States. It is 603 kilometers or 375 miles from the border to New York City, 814 kilometers or 505.8 miles to Washington, DC and 629 kilometers or 391 miles to Boston, Massachusetts.

If you are coming east from Vancouver, it is 4,363 kilometers or 2,711 miles via the United States to cut mileage. Coming west from Toronto it is 406.5 kilometers or 253 miles. And from Montréal it is only 197 kilometers or 122.4 miles.

Arriving in Ottawa by expressway

* If you are flying into Canada from the United States, you will find that several major American carriers fly from the many major American cities to Ottawa's Macdonald-Cartier International Airport, which is very close to the center of the

city. But the most widespread service is offered by Air Canada or WestJet, which are always my recommendation. Ottawa also has connecting overseas air service offered by several international airlines with service between Dublin, London Heathrow, Paris, Amsterdam, Frankfurt, Zurich and Rome, connecting through Montréal. Because of Ottawa's close proximity to Montréal, it would not pay for the airlines to offer duplicated service.

Macdonald-Cartier International Airport, (Work of P199, CC BY SA 3.0, Wikimedia.org)

* Passenger rail service into Ottawa is quite extensive, connecting the city with both Toronto and Montréal. There are numerous daily trains between Toronto's Union Station and Ottawa's main station. The sole provider is Via Rail Canada, the country's national rail service. A journey takes approximately four hours and there are two classes of service – Coach and Via One, which is outstanding with complimentary hot meals and bar service. There are also numerous trains each day between Ottawa and Gare Central in downtown Montréal. This journey takes just under two hours and both Coach and Via One service are offered. Visit online with www.viarail.ca for details.

In Toronto passengers can connect with the "Canadian," the long distance overland service to and from Vancouver. And in Montréal passengers can connect with the "Ocean," overnight service to Halifax.

In both Toronto and Montréal passengers can also connect with the American passenger rail network for service to New York, and from Toronto also to Chicago. Visit online with www.amtrak.com for details.

Two Via Rail day trains about to depart Ottawa, (Work of David Wilsson, CC BY SA 2.0, Wikimedia.org)

GETTING TO YOUR HOTEL

FROM OTTAWA'S MACDONALD-CARTIER INTERNATIONAL AIRPORT: Ottawa's international airport is 22 kilometers or 14 miles. There are only four viable options for visitors with luggage. These options are:

* Private airport transfer service can be arranged through all major four and five-star hotels. Average fares into the city center are $60.00 plus any gratuity. There are airport dispatchers to guide you to your limo after collecting your luggage and passing through customs. Porter service is available in the baggage hall if you need it.

* Hotel shuttles may be available provided by your hotel. Before making any private arrangements, check with your hotel to see if they offer airport shuttle service. The major four and five-star hotels do not offer shuttle service, but rather will offer limousine service through a contracted provider. The average cost for the transfer service is $80 to $100 plus gratuities.

One of many taxi companies in Ottawa

* Taxis are available outside the arrivals hall at the airport and also outside the main terminal at Ottawa's Via Rail station. There are several taxi services and shuttles. The fare into the city center will be around $30 dollars or more from either the airport or the railway station. And yes tipping is expected in Canada. For taxi service a ten percent tip is customary, especially if the driver assists you with your luggage.

* City bus service is provided between downtown Ottawa and the airport, but it is not convenient for passengers with luggage. For details visit online with www.octranspo.com . OC Transpo also does offer city bus service between the Via Rail Station and downtown. Both airport or railway station routes to downtown take half an hour with many stops. If you have anything larger than a small flight bag it will be very cumbersome for you to utilize a city bus.

DRIVING: If you are driving into Ottawa directly from the United States you most likely will be crossing the border between Ogdensburg, New York and Prescott, Ontario. Refer back to page 54 for distance details. It will take approximately two hours after clearing border formalities to arrive in the city center. I do not recommend driving unless you are comfortable with bilingual road signs and distances given in kilometers only. Traffic in Ottawa is not as difficult to navigate as in Toronto or Montréal, but there are morning and evening rush hours that can be demanding upon your patience, especially after a long flight. Parking in the city center is limited and also expensive. Most hotels offer parking for guests and at the major hotels you will pay around $30 to $35 per day for parking plus gratuities each time you take the car out.

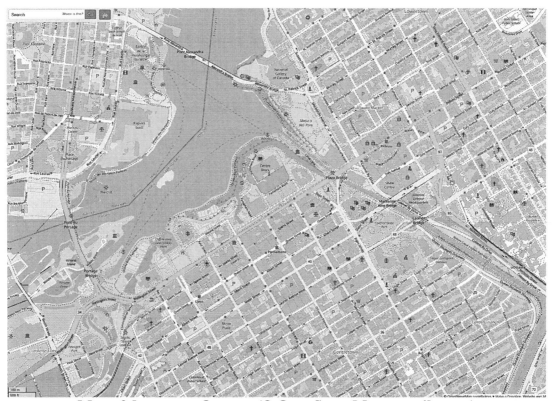

Map of downtown Ottawa, (© OpenStreetMap contributors)

ACCOMMODATION

Ottawa does have many fine hotels, but unlike Vancouver or Toronto it does not offer an abundance of four or five star properties. Most visitors are short term guests and are either in the city on government or private business. The remainder are staying a few days for sightseeing purposes.

Most visitors choose to be in the city center, as this is the heart of all the important activities, dining, shopping, theater, sports and nightlife. If you stay out in the suburbs, you then miss so much of the excitement and flavor of being in Ottawa. Although there is good public transit, Ottawa is quite spread out, and a good portion of the urban zone is located across the Ottawa River in the province of Québec where you will run into the language issue. On the Québec side of the river where there are numerous attractions be prepared to find fewer people who will offer their services initially in English. But the vast majority will speak English but only upon request.

To not show any favoritism, I have listed the hotels alphabetically, but I have also added my personal views as to what they have to offer regarding their location and amenities. These are my Ottawa choices:

* ALT HOTEL: At 185 Slater Street, this very modern hotel offers superb rooms and services within the heart of thee downtown core. The hotel does offer a trendy café, fitness center and facilities, but it does not have guest parking. For details visit www.germainhotels.com/alt-hotel . I give it ***

* ANDAZ OTTAWA BYWARD MARKET: This Andaz by Hyatt is an ideal hotel located in thee Byward Market area at 325 Dalhousie Street. It offers beautiful rooms and suites with the corner accommodation having spectacular views from the upper floors. Complimentary breakfast is offered and there is a full service dining room as well as banquet service. The hotel offers full concierge service, a fitness center and business center as well as a garage with valet service. For full details visit www.hyatt.com .I GIVE IT ****

* BUSINESS INN & SUITES (THE): This modern high rise hotel is at 180 Maclaren Street at the corner of Elgin Street. This is a good property for extended stays, as it does offer outfitted kitchen facilities in many suites. Free buffet breakfast is provided but there is no dining service. There is paid parking but no valet service. For details visit www.thebusinessinn.com .I GIVE IT *** .

* DELTA HOTELS BY MARRIOTT OTTAWA CITY CENTRE: The Delta hotel chain is found in every major Canadian downtown. The hotel in Ottawa is located at It is located at 101 Lyon Street North and offers full services, as to be expected from a major hotel. The hotel offers a variety of rooms and suites, those with high floors often having excellent views. The hotel offers a fitness center and pool, gift shop,

restaurant, room service, meeting and banquet rooms and indoor parking. For full details visit www.marriott.com .I GIVE IT ****

Delta Hotel Ottawa Centre, (Work of Jeangagnon, CC BY SA 4.0, Wikimedia.org)

* FAIRMONT CHATEAU LAURIER: The most famous hotel in Ottawa is the castle adjacent to Parliament Hill that shows up on thousands of photos of the city. This castle is the Chateau Laurier, one of the grand Canadian hotels built by the railroads in the days before automobile dominance.

The Chateau Laurier, today a proud Fairmont property is the epitome of five-star luxury and elegance in Ottawa. If you want the finest in accommodation and service and are able to afford the tariff, there is no place finer than this incredibly magnificent hotel. They have a wide array of rooms and suites, superb dining rooms and all of the services you expect from a five-star hotel. For full details visit www.fairmont.com/laurier . Without question I GIVE IT ****

The Chateau Laurier, (Work of Jeangagnon, CC BY SA 4.0, Wikimedia.org)

* HOMEWOOD SUITES BY HILTON DOWNTOWN: At 361 Queen Street, this is a high rise hotel offering complimentary breakfast, a fitness center and pool and paid parking without valet. This is a basic hotel but one with excellent quality. For details visit www.homewoodsuites3.hilton.com . I GIVE IT ***

* LE GERMAIN HOTEL: This rather modern hotel is located close to the downtown core and Parliament Hill. It is at 30 Daly Avenue, which is in the heart of the downtown vibe. The hotel offers a variety of smart rooms and suites, has a dining room, room service, both a fitness and business center and offers valet parking. Courtesy car service is offered within the immediate vicinity of the downtown core. For details visit www.germainhotels.com/le-germain GIVE IT ****

* LE SUITES HOTEL OTTAWA: Located close to Parliament Hill at 130 Besserer Street, this all-suite hotel offers affordable luxury with excellent and spacious suites rather than a cramped hotel room. There is a café offering breakfast and light fare during the day, but no full hot meals. However, kitchen equipped suites are offered and great for long term stays. Fitness room and a both a pool and hot tub are offered, and business facilities are provided. There is indoor parking but a fee is charged. Visit on line at www.les-suites.com for details. I GIVE IT ****

* LORD ELGIN HOTEL: Facing out to the Rideau Canal at 100 Elgin Street, this venerable hotel is one of the long time established properties in the heart of the city. Guest rooms are updated to the latest in modern comforts while retaining a classic look. The main dining room offers all meals of the day served in a traditional

elegant atmosphere. Traditional room service is provided. There is also a Starbucks in the hotel. A business center and gift shop add to the convenience as does valet parking. The hotel also offers meeting, conference and business services. Visit on line at www.lordelginhotel.ca for details. I GIVE IT ****

The Lord Elgin Hotel, (Work of Joan Clifford, CC BY SA 2.0, Wikimedia.org)

Marriott Ottawa Hotel seen from afar

* OTTAWA MARRIOTT HOTEL: This downtown Marriott is at 100 Kent Street, easily recognized by its revolving restaurant high atop the building. This is a full service Marriott with a variety of room and suite types, restaurants, room service, an indoor pool, fitness center, business enter and concierge. The hotel also has meeting and banquet facilities. The revolving restaurant atop the hotel does afford excellent views of the city and Parliament Hill. Valet parking is available as well as self-service. For details visit www.marriott.com . I GIVE IT ****

* SHERATON OTTAWA: The downtown Sheraton at 150 Albert Street offers its guests all the amenities that are typical of major Sheraton hotels. Comfortable guest rooms and suites are traditional and somewhat basic. The hotel offers a main dining room as well as room service. There is a fitness center, indoor pool, a small convenience store and both self and valet parking. Visit them at www.marriott.com for details. I GIVE IT ***

* WESTIN HOTEL OTTAWA: The Westin Hotel is an outstanding facility located along the Rideau Canal at the corner of Rideau Street and Sussex Drive. It is attached to the very major downtown Rideau Centre, one of Ottawa's largest shopping malls. And via the Rideau Center, the hotel is also linked to the downtown Hudson's Bay Company and Byward Market. The Westin offers a variety of top accommodation, their premium rooms being the ones on the northwest corner with a commanding view of Parliament Hill. Superb dining, a fitness center and pool and all business and conference facilities are provided. Visit www.marriott.com for full details. I GIVE IT ****

Westin Hotel Ottawa, (Work of Simon P, CC BY SA 3.0, Wikimedia.org)

GETTING AROUND

SEEING THE CITY: The greater Ottawa community is spread out and bifurcated by the wide Ottawa River. The Ontario side of the river is home to the main city of Ottawa along with numerous suburban communities that spread out along the southern bank of the river. On the Québec north shore are the cities of Hull and Gatineau, now unified, plus numerous smaller communities both along the river and stretching inland to the north.

What adds to the overall size of the urban area is the amount of parkland devoted to preserving the natural environment, or surrounding various government buildings or simply beautifying such features as the Rideau Canal, the Rideau River and the Gatineau River. Also on the Québec side the Gatineau Park is a very significant green belt that stretches north for many kilometers.

The vast parklands on the Québec side of the Ottawa River, (© OpenStreetMap contributors)

The city core of Ottawa does exhibit dozens of high rise apartments and condominium, giving it a heavy concentration of residents. But in contrast to other major Canadian cities, the bulk of residential Ottawa and also Gatineau is dominated over by single family homes, making the city feel more open, but also consuming a lot of ground. The bottom line for visitors is the need to get around and explore all that it has to offer.

The concentration of parks in the City of Ottawa's core ((© OpenStreetMap contributors)

OPTIONS FOR EXPLORING GREATER OTTAWA: Here are the options available for exploring greater Ottawa and the many outlying sights in both province:

* **Private car and driver service** – This is the best option for exploring the sights of Ottawa and its surroundings. Having a private car and driver gives you the greatest degree of flexibility, as the driver is at your disposal at all times. Here are the companies I recommend for private touring, most of them being the same ones your hotel concierge would arrange for your use.

** www.toursbylocals/Ottawa-tours is a very good provider for tours on a private one on one basis.

** www.tourtravelandmore.com is a very reliable company for organizing both small group and private tours.

** www.getyourguide.com/ottawa-ottawa1285 offers personalized tours from one to six hours in length.

* **Car rental service** – Either at the airport or at your hotel you can make arrangements with all of the national car rental agencies for a personal car to use while in Ottawa. The only negative about driving your own rental car is finding your way around. And in the city center where many important venues are located you will find parking to be quite limited.

Many people do not find it easy to enjoy relaxed sightseeing while having to be their own driver. Ottawa streets are quite wide and well designed and there is an expressway system. But you will still face the normal problems of driving and parking in a large city as you would anywhere in Canada or for that matter in the world.

Also when you cross the Ottawa River to do any touring on the Québec side of the river you will find that all road and information signs are written only in French.

* **Taxi touring** is another option that your hotel concierge can arrange. Taxi touring is not as comfortable and the drivers may not be as capable in serving as tour guides. It can be hit or miss, but it is far less expensive than private touring.

One major taxi touring service is Executive Cabs and Limousine Services. Visit their web page at www.executivecabs.ca for details.

* **Group tours** can be arranged by your hotel concierge, or you can contact the companies I list below. These are motor coach or small van tours that are pre-established with an itinerary where you have little to no chance to customize the venues. The following tour companies can be contacted on your own if you prefer.

** www.ottawatourism.ca/ottawa-insider/guided-tours is one of the major sources for group tours of the sights of Ottawa.

** www.ottawavalleytours.com is a major provider of pre set group tours.

** www.viatour.com/things-to-do/ottawa provides information on short group tours across the country.

* **Hop on Hop Off Bus** – This is one inexpensive way to tour around in the city of Ottawa. Here are the major providers:

** www.hop-on-hop-off-bus.com/ottawa is the major Gray Line provider in the city of Ottawa.

* **Walking** is an option if you want to stay in the city center or around the neighborhood where your hotel is located if not in the city center. For individuals who do not wish to explore far beyond the hotel, this is an acceptable option, but rather limiting.

* **OC Transpo** – This is the public bus company that serves the city of Ottawa. They offer personalized information regarding how to tour around the city and also provide fare details. There is a second line called Line Two Trillium but as of 2022 it has been closed for further construction. Visit on line at www.octranspo.com for assistance.

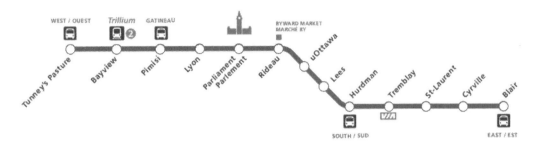

A map of the current Line One of the OC Transpo train

The OC Transpo train, (Work of Youngjiin, CC BY SA 3.0, Wikimedia.org)

* Walking is one of the best ways to enjoy Ottawa. By combining public transport with your own feet, you can explore many neighborhoods, visit important venues and also enjoy the city's parks. Your hotel concierge will provide maps and help you plan walking tours, and I will have more ideas when I discuss the major sights of the city. And the grounds around Parliament Hill should best be enjoyed on foot.

SIGHTS TO SEE

When is the best time to visit Ottawa? From April, as the snow begins to melt away through the summer and into the magnificent fall when the leaves put on a brilliant display Ottawa is at its best. Winter is also beautiful for those who enjoy the vigorous chill of the season. And there is a scenic quality to winter unmatched by any other season. But for the vast majority of potential visitors, it is simply too cold.

Late spring is still cool to sometimes chilly, but when the tulips begin to bloom in May, they bring a dazzling display of multi colors to the city parks. Since the end of World War II the government of the Netherlands has been gifting one million tulip bulbs to the city for having sheltered the crown princess during World War II, and the city matches the gift. It is quite a spectacle.

Summer is essentially quite comfortable because of the more northerly latitude, but there can be very warm and humid days. But heat waves in Ottawa are actually quite rare.

The Peace Tower on Parliament Hill framed in fall colors

Fall is absolutely the choice time to visit Ottawa and its surroundings. The fall colors in the Gatineau Hills and throughout the city are breathtaking. This is a very popular time to visit and hotels book up early. The same conditions apply all along the St. Lawrence River and into the Atlantic Provinces to the east and in the province of Ontario mainly around Toronto.

Winter is very cold and the snow can pile up quickly, but it offers its own beauty. If you are one of those people like me who loves snow, the city draped in white is very striking. And for skaters, the frozen Rideau Canal offers the world's longest ice skating rink. The entire length of the canal within the city becomes a skating rink that is approximately 10 kilometers long.

WHAT TO SEE AND DO: The many of major sites that visitors to Ottawa must see while visiting the city are for the most part clustered close together in the

* BANK OF CANADA MUSEUM – This is a museum that exhibits all of the variations in Canadian currency dating back to colonial times. For anyone interested in the evolution of the Canadian Dollar, this is a must see venue. For most visitors, it is a museum that holds little interest. Due to Covid the museum has been closed. You need to visit www.bankofcanadamuseum.ca to see if it is open when you wish to visit.

* BYWARD MARKET – The Byward Market is located just to the east of Parliament Hill, occupying a couple of square blocks, offering a great variety of fruits, vegetables, meats, seafood and handcraft items. It is a traditional public market made up of 500 different vendors. The market opens daily at 9 AM and most vendors close at 5 PM. For visitors this is one of the best places to buy maple syrup and other confections made from this sweet tree sap. It is so traditional a gift for people to bring back from Canada.

Byward Market

* CANADA AVIATION AND SPACE MUSEUM – For those with a of aviation this is a venue not to be missed. The exhibits chronicle the national aviation history of Canada. It is located at 11 Aviation Parkway in the Rockcliffe Airport, which will require your own or public transport to reach. The museum is open Thursday thru Monday between 9 AM and 5 PM. For more specific details visit the web page at www.ingeniumcanada.org for details.

* CANADA SCIENCE AND TECHNOLOGY MUSEUM – This is the nation's premier museum of science and technology, promoting the history and heritage of the field of scientific investigation in Canada. The museum is located at 1867 St. Laurent Boulevard, which will require private transportation for you to reach if on your own and not part of a tour. Museum hours are from 9 AM to 5 PM Wednesday thru Sunday. Visit on line at www.ingeniumcanada.org/scitech for full details.

* CANADIAN MUSEUM OF HISTORY – This is Canada's museum of anthropology and cultural history, housed in a spectacular modern building in Gatineau at 100 Laurier Street. The museum occupies the once ugly site of a massive lumber mill. Today its magnificent architecture compliments that of Parliament Hill, which it faces. It is within walking distance from the heart of the city via the Alexandra Bridge. The museum hours are from 9 AM to 4 PM Wednesday thru Sunday with extended closing at 7 PM on Wednesday. For more details visit on line at www.historymuseum.ca for full details.

Canadian Museum of History, (Work of Michel Rathwell, CC BY SA 2.0, Wikimedia.org)

* **CANADIAN MUSEUM OF NATURE** – This is Canada's national museum of natural history. The exhibits, which feature exhibits on all aspects of the country's diverse environments is located at 240 McLeod Street, which is just to the south of the downtown core, a fair, but not difficult walk from most major hotels. The museum hours are from 9 AM to 4 PM Wednesday thru Sunday with extended closing at 7 PM on Wednesday. For more details visit on line at www.nature.ca .

* **CANADIAN TULIP FESTIVAL** – Each year in the middle of May the city of Ottawa comes alive with the glorious blooming of thousands of tulips planted in all of the public parks of Ottawa and Gatineau. During World War II the government hosted the Crown Princess of Netherlands to keep her safe. As a tribute and thank you each year the Dutch people send one million tulip bulbs, which the city matches to produce a world famous display of these fragile blooms. The festival begins two weeks prior to Victoria Day, so if you wish to book a visit do it early at over 600,000 visitors come. Victoria Day is the fourth Monday in May so you can plan accordingly. Visit on line at www.tulipfestival.ca for details.

One of the many tulip beds during the festival in May< (Work of Paul Shannon, CC BY SA 2.5, Wikimedia.org)

* **CANADIAN WAR MUSEUM** – Canada has been a participant in numerous global and regional conflicts since becoming a nation in 1867. Prior to independence, Canada was a British Colony and also saw its share of continental

military actions with the United States. This museum exhibits artifacts and chronicles the history of warfare for Canada. The museum is located at One Vimy Place along the Ottawa River approximately two kilometers west of Parliament Hill. It is essentially a long, but doable walk from most downtown hotels. Hours are between 9 AM and 4 PM Wednesday thru Sunday with a 7 PM closing on Thursday. Visit www.warmuseum.ca for specific details.

* GATINEAU PARK – The Gatineau Hills are a series of rocky outcrops that extend north from the Ottawa River on the Québec side, offering thick woodland and glacial lakes covering 361 square kilometers or 139 square miles. Most of the park is original wilderness that offers an array of activities within the greater urban environment. Its abrupt rise presents an escarpment facing south that also offers spectacular views of the Ottawa River Valley. The park is open to visitors daily form 9 AM to 4 PM with 5 PM closing on Saturday and Sunday. During the fall this is one of the best places within the urban area to enjoy the brilliant fall colors. Visit on line at www.ncc-ccn.gc.ca for details

Gatineau Park in late fall, (Work of cjuneau, CC BY SA 2.0, Wikimedia.org)

* LAURIER HOUSE NATIONAL HISTORIC SITE – This national historic museum was used by two of Canada's early prime ministers in the years before 24 Sussex Drive was commissioned as the official residence. It is located at 335 Laurier Avenue East in the central city core. For specific details since the closure due to Covid 19, visit on line at www.pc.gc.ca/en/lhn-nhs/on/laurier for details and current hours.

* MACKENZIE KING ESTATE – This beautifully preserved Victorian Era country estate was once home to Prime Minister Mackenzie King who was the longest serving leader of Canada. It is located on Mackenzie King Road in Chelsea, a suburban neighborhood in Gatineau, Québec. You will need to have your own transportation to get there, but it is worth the effort.

It is open Wednesday thru Monday from 10 AM to 5 PM with later closing Saturday and Sunday at 6 PM. Visit on line at www.ncc-ccn.gc.ca/places/mackenzie-king -estate for full details.

Mackenzie King Estate

* MEECH LAKE – This small glacial lake is found in the upper reaches of Gatineau Park. It is one of many such lakes, but to Canadians who are history fans, the lake is famous as the site where the later failed Meech Lake Accord was drafted. In 1987 then Prime Minister Mulroney attempted to secure an agreement from all of the provinces regarding special status for Québec during the time when there was strong sentiment for separation from Canada. The vote by the public failed to accept the accord.

The park visitor center will need to give you directions on finding the lake. Again you will definitely need your own transportation to reach this gem of a lake, as it is quite secluded and accessed by a narrow back lane that is not sealed. Visit on line at www.ncc-ccn.gc.ca/places/meech-lake for details.

Meech Lake, (Work of LBM1948, CC BY SA 4.0, Wikimedia.org)

**The National Gallery of Canada, (Work of Jeangagnon, CC BY SA 4.0,
Wikimedia.org)**

* NATIONAL GALLERY OF CANADA – The National Gallery of Canada is housed in one of the most dramatic buildings in all of Ottawa. It is a very modern and almost futuristic construct, located at 380 Sussex Drive on the corner where traffic to and from Gatineau via the Alexandra Bridge intersects. The gallery stands high above the Ottawa River and is very visible from the Québec side of the river as one of the principal skyline icons. This gallery offers the greatest collection of indigenous and 19th century Canadian art. It offers a wide array of artifacts, sculptures and paintings that chronicle the history of art in Canada. Featured are many works by the Group of Seven, a turn of the century collection of artists who created a very distinct style of painting that still influences Canadian artists of today. The gallery is open Wednesday thru Sunday from 10 AM to 5 PM and should be on every visitor's list of places to visit. You can tour the gallery web pages at www.gallery.ca for more details.

The magnificent National War Memorial

* NATIONAL WAR MEMORIAL – Occupying a triangular plot of ground in the heart of Ottawa where Wellington Street and Elgin Street meet. The memorial sits in the center of this triangular wedge that is known as Confederation Square. In front of the memorial sits the Tomb of the Unknown Soldier. And combined these two monuments are considered to be hallowed ground. It is here that the national Remembrance Day ceremonies are held each November 11th, drawing thousands of people all sporting their red poppy, symbolic of the conclusion of World War I. The memorial is always open. For details visit www.veterans.gc.ca .

* NOTRE DAME BASILICA – Located at 385 Sussex Drive just opposite the National Gallery of Canada is the magnificent Notre Dame Basilica, home to the Roman Catholic Archdiocese of Ottawa. It has been designated as a National Historic Site for its grand architecture in the Québécois tradition. It was built in 1846 in what is called a Gothic Revival or Neoclassical style., Visitors are welcome Tuesday thru Friday from 11:45 AM to 1 PM, Saturday from 4:30 to 6 PM and on Sunday between 9:30 AM and 1 PM and again between 4:30 and 6 PM. Visit the web pages at www.notredameottawa.com for details.

Notre Dame Basilica in fall

* PARLIAMENT HILL – Overlooking the Ottawa River from its high bluff, and facing on to Wellington Street is the focal hub of the Canadian Government. The collection of magnificent buildings is collectively known as Parliament Hill. This is where the legislature of the nation known as Parliament meets for its debates and where many of the offices of government leaders are to be found. The most dramatic building is the Centre Block, which is dominated over by the Peace Tower, still the tallest structure in Ottawa. The architecture of the three main buildings, the

Centre Block, East and West Blocks are very similar to that of the Palace of Westminster, the home of the British Parliament in London.

Visitors can enter the main Centre Block on weekdays between 8:30 AM and 5 PM where both the upper house known as the Senate and the more powerful lower house known as the House of Commons hold their debates . Both the exterior and interior of the buildings reflect a Gothic style of architecture. For details visit www.canada.ca/attractions-canada-capital/parliament for details.

The Centre Block of Parliament seen through the royal gate only opened for the Monarch on state visits

* RIDEAU CANAL NATIONAL HISTORIC SITE –This mid 19th century canal connects the city of Ottawa with Lake Ontario at Kingston, a 202 kilometer or 125 mile waterway with numerous sets of locks to raise and lower small boats during the transit. Today it is used primarily by pleasure craft, and through the city of Ottawa the canal is beautifully landscaped, crossed by many important bridges and also overlooked by such important buildings as Parliament, the Chateau Laurier, the Department of National Defence, the Lord Elgin Hotel and many other landmark structures.

During winter once the water freezes, it is prepped and maintained in the city as the world's longest ice skating rink. The winter activities draw locals and visitors alike, making this working canal a source of recreation as well as commerce.

For information on the importance, operation and historic sites along the way, visit on line at www.pc.gc.ca/ihn-nhs/rideau for full details.

Winter skaters on the Rideau Canal, (Work of Nairg, CC BY SA 3.0, Wikimedia.org)

* RIDEAU CENTRE – This is the major downtown shopping mall serving the city center. There are skyways that connect the Rideau Centre with Nordstrom, Hudson's Bay Company and other important venues. In addition to choice shopping, Rideau Center offers dining and entertainment venues. Hours of service are Monday thru Saturday from 10 AM to 8 PM and Sunday from 11 AM to 6 PM. Visit the center's web pages at www.shops.cadillacfairview.com/cf-rideau-centre for details.

* RIDEAU FALLS – The Rideau River is a major tributary to the Ottawa River, flowing from the interior lake district of southern Ontario. The final drop of two eleven meter waterfalls separated by an island occurs when the Rideau River plunges over the steep bank of the Ottawa River. The parkland alongside the eastern shore combined with the government buildings on Green Island between the two falls makes this a visually stunning part of the city landscape. The overviews in the park are always open to the public.

* RIDEAU HALL – Keep in mind that the Canadian government is a constitutional monarchy, but the King or Queen of Canada is the same person who is also the head of the British nation and 14 other Commonwealth countries. Thus each of the member nations apart from the United Kingdom selects a Governor General to represent the Crown. The official residence in Canada for the Governor General and the monarch during state visits is Rideau Hall. It is essentially Canada's Royal Palace.

The grounds are open to the public except during times when official functions are held. And certain public rooms within Rideau Hall are also open. Hours are between 8 and 4:30 PM daily, but you must secure a reservation for the interior visit in advance. Visit on line for details or to secure space at www.gg.ca/visit-us/rideau-hall to finalize details.

Rideau Hall, (Work of Concierge2C, CC BY SA 3.0, Wikimedia.org)

* ROYAL CANADIAN MINT – The mint is located in the heart of the city at 320 Sussex Drive. This is the main focus of where Canadian coins are produced along with medals and other important commemorative objects. The mint is not responsible for producing paper currency, and that facility is not a regular tourist attraction.

Tours of the Royal Canadian Mint are offered but must be booked in advance. The mint is open Wednesday thru Sunday from 10 AM to 5 PM. To book a tour visit on line at www.mint.ca .

The Royal Canadian Mint, (Work of Skeezix1000, CC BY SA 3.0, Wikimedia.org)

Tomb of the Unknown Soldier in front of the War Memorial

* TOMB OF THE UNKNOWN SOLDIER – Many countries honor their fallen soldiers, but Canada's Tomb of the Unknown Soldier is appropriately placed at the foot of the national war memorial in the very heart of Ottawa. Occupying a place of sacred honor, on Remembrance Day (November 11) at the end of the ceremony it is customary for those in attendance to place their red paper poppy, symbolizing World War I sacrifices, atop the Tomb of the Unknown Soldier. It is a very emotional and touching scene. The monument and tomb are always open to the public,

*NOTE: There are many more venues of interest in the greater Ottawa vicinity, but what I have listed in this chapter are those of greatest significance or interest to visitors. For even greater detail, I recommend an on line visit to www.tripadvisor.com where you will find a total listing of points of interest in and around Ottawa.

DINING OUT

When it comes to dining out in greater Ottawa, a city that offers both fine traditional Canadian and international dining. Given its location on the border with Québec, there is a great variety from which to choose within the category of Canadian cuisine. Much of Canada's fine gastronomy has been heavily influenced by the culture of Québec. Here the early French settlers at the start of the 17th century had to adapt their recipes from France to local ingredients, many of which were totally new to them. The end result was what visitors often simply call French cuisine, but in reality it is Québécois cuisine – uniquely Canadian.

This chapter is intended to present the best of what greater Ottawa has to offer when it comes to a variety of excellent foods, as it is easy to simply follow the crowds and not have a memorable experience.

In all Canadian cities so many small, intimate restaurants exist in every shopping district, this being especially true in the most major cities. But here in the Ottawa region visitors often overlook local inns or restaurants in the neighboring small towns of Ontario and the rural countryside of Québec. There is a great variety of gastronomy to be enjoyed, but to fully seek it out requires having access to private transportation.

I am only listing a select number of recommended restaurants in both Ottawa and Gatineau alphabetically in three categories; Places to Dine for Breakfast or Lunch, Fine Evening Dining and Desserts:

PLACES TO DINE FOR BREAKFAST OR LUNCH: There are so many restaurants crowding the city center and in neighboring Hull-Gatineau across the Ottawa River in Québec.

Do not overlook the buffet breakfast found in most of the four and five star hotels that I have already listed in the accommodation category. Hotel breakfast in Canada is often far superior to what is found in other countries.

My choices for Ottawa and Hull-Gatineau morning and midday dining are:

* CORA'S BREAKFAST & LUNCH – Located in the Byward Market area at 179 Rideau Street, this very popular downtown eatery offers outstanding breakfast and lunch dishes in the Canadian tradition. The menu is very diverse and features favorites not often seen. The menu is also vegetarian friendly. Hours of service are daily from 6 AM to 3 PM. Reservations are not necessary.

* DALY'S RESTAURANT – This is the main dining room at the Westin Ottawa hotel, and it is a fine, yet casual place for breakfast and early lunch. Their menu is diverse, but with a distinct Canadian flair. And they also offer very fine desserts in

the afternoon and evening. Weekday service is form 7 to 11 AM extended closing at 11;30 AM on weekends. Call 613 560 7000 to book a table.

* GRILL 41 – This is the very popular main dining room at the Lord Elgin Hotel, and has been a popular dining establishment for many decades. The atmosphere contemporary and is considered as quite smart. The cuisine is Canadian with international touches, offering a wide array of dishes. The restaurant serves breakfast and dinner and is open daily from 6 to 10 AM and from 5 to 10 PM. Call 613 569 2126 to book a table.

* LE FOUGERES – Located in the village of Tenaga, which is a part of Chelsea, Québec. The actual location is 783 Route 105. This is personally one of my favorites in the greater Ottawa region and has been for decades. Their menu is traditional with fine quality Canadian and French dishes. And the service is always very gracious. They are open Wednesday thru Friday from 11:30 AM to 9 PM and on weekends from 10 AM to 9:30 PM Call to book a table at 819 827 8942.

Winter at Le Fougeres, (Compliments of Le Fougeres)

* PELICAN SEAFOOD MARKET AND GRILL – This is one of Ottawa's most popular seafood restaurants with fresh catches available daily. They are located at 1500 Bank Street in the Blue Heron Mall. It is a few kilometers south of downtown so you will need a taxi or your own transportation. They serve lunch and dinner daily from 11:30 AM to 8:30 PM with a 9:30 PM closing on Friday and Saturday. Call 613 526 5229 to book a table.

* PURE KITCHEN ELGIN – At 340 Elgin Street in the downtown core, this is a restaurant that specializes in vegetarian and vegan cuisine expertly prepared and beautifully served. They serve breakfast, lunch and dinner daily from 8 AM to 10 PM daily with two modifications – On Sunday they open at 9 AM and close at 9 PM and on Saturday they open at 9 AM rather than at 8 AM. Call 613 233 7873 to see you need to book a table.

* SHORE CLUB – This is a casual dining room at the Westin Ottawa hotel where fine quality fresh seafood and outstanding steaks are the specialty. Their menu does offer a variety of complimentary side dishes. Hours of service are Sunday and Monday from 3 to 11 PM and Tuesday thru Saturday from 3 PM to Midnight. Wednesday thru Friday they serve from 11:30 AM to Midnight. Call 612 5660 7000 to book a table.

* WILD OAT (THE) – This popular restaurant for breakfast and lunch is located at 817 Bank Street just south of the downtown core by two kilometer. It serves traditional Canadian breakfast and lunch dishes that are excellent and quite filling. Their menu offers great variety including vegetarian dishes and is very popular with locals. They also are open for dinner. Their hours are daily from 7 AM to 8 PM and reservations are not necessary.

* ZOE'S – This is a more casual, yet elegant dining room inside the Chateau Laurier in the heart of Ottawa. Both lunch and dinner are served in an elegant, yet relaxed atmosphere. Both the cuisine and service live up to the ongoing high level of the hotel. The hours are daily from 11 AM to 11 PM and reservations are essential. Call 613 241 1414.

FINE EVENING DINING: As the national capital city, Ottawa is well endowed with fine quality restaurants offering the finest in elegant dining. And for those who want a more casual evening meal there are also an equal number of less expensive, but still fine quality restaurants. My choices in Ottawa and Gatineau are:

* ABSINTHE – This outstanding restaurant offers up a superb Canadian traditional cuisine, but also offers many other ethnic selections. Quality and service are excellent. They always receive rave reviews for their quality and ambiance. The location is 1208 Wellington Street West, which is a few kilometers south and west of downtown. You will need to use a taxi or have your own transportation, but it is worth the short drive. Dinner is served daily from 5 to 10 PM. Reservations can be made by calling 613 761 1138.

* 1 ELGIN – Located in the National Arts Centre at 1 Elgin Street, this is a very well respected and popular place for an elegant evening dinner overlooking the Rideau Canal. Both the cuisine and service are excellent and the menu is Canadian and international in its offering. Their serving hours are from 5 to 9 PM Tuesday thru Saturday. Reservations are required and can be made at 613 594 5127.

* ATELIER - Located at 540 Rochester Street near Dow's Lake, this fine dining establishment will be too far to walk from the downtown core. Their international menu with strong Canadian touches features a wide array of dishes elegantly prepared and served to please the most discriminating diner. They serve only dinner from 5 to 10 PM Tuesday thru Saturday. Reservations are essential and can be made at 613 321 3537.

* BECKTA DINING & WINE – This is a beautiful dining room with an old world flavor. It is located at i50 Elgin Street in the historic Grant House with its Victorian Era details. Their diverse menu offers a wide range of dishes and also a tasting menu to broaden one's horizons. Their serving hours are 5 to 10 PM Tuesday thru Saturday. Reservations are necessary by calling 613 238 7063.

* CHEZ FATIMA – For a taste treat from Morocco and the Mediterranean, this popular restaurant is an ideal place for a new experience. The menu selections include vegetarian and Halal dishes served in a pleasant atmosphere. The address is 125 Promenade du Portage, in Gatineau. This will necessitate either a taxi or your own transportation. Lunch is served weekdays from 11:30 AM to 2 PM and dinner is served daily from 5:30 to 9:30 PM Call 819 771 7568 to book a table.

* FRASER – Here is a very well known and popular Canadian restaurant with a diverse menu of what can be called comfort food. It is located at 7 Springfield Road across the Rideau River a short distance from downtown. Their hours of service are daily from 5 to 10 PM. Call 613 749 1444 to book a table.

* GEZELLIG – Located about four kilometers southwest of the city center, you will need to use a taxi or your own vehicle to reach this superb restaurant at 337 Richmond Street. This is a fine dining establishment with a menu that combines Canadian and international dishes. The quality of the cuisine and level of service make this one of Ottawa's fine dining establishments. The do also offer vegetarian dishes as well as an array of meat, poultry and seafood entrees. Reservations are necessary by calling 613 680 9086. Serving hours are Wednesday thru Friday from 5 to 9 PM, Saturday and Sunday from 10 AM to 2 PM as well as 5 to 10 PM.

* HUNTER'S PUBLIC HOUSE RESTAURANT – This is a very good Canadian restaurant in which fresh seafood is the specialty despite being in Ottawa. Fresh catches are flown in and prepared in the Atlantic style found in places like Halifax. Their hours are with an opening at 11 AM daily, closing at 9 PM Sunday thru Wednesday , closing at 11 PM Thursday and Midnight on Friday and Saturday. Call them at 613 822 7171 to see if you need to reserve a table.

* LE BACCARA – This elegant restaurant is located at 1 boulevard du Casino and is one of the most popular places to enjoy fine quality Québécois and international cuisine. I have enjoyed the restaurant on all my visits to greater Ottawa. The quality of the cuisine and the level of service are superb. However, when reading their reviews you will find that many English speaking reviewers have made disparaging

comments about both the "snob" appeal and the prices. So my recommendation is aimed at those who like the French manner and do not take offense at a bit of snob appeal. I personally have always enjoyed it. To book a table call 819 772 6210.

* SANSOTEI RAMEN – This is a well known Japanese restaurant specializing in ramen dishes that are freshly made, served piping hot and are delicious. Even for those not familiar with Japanese cuisine, ramen is one dish that always pleases. The restaurant is downtown at 153 Bank Street. Their hours are 11 AM to 10 PM daily. Call to see if you need a reservation at 613 695 1718.

* SUPPLY AND DEMAND FOODS & RAW BAR – At 1335 Wellington Street West, you will need your own transportation or a taxi to dine here, but it is well worth the effort for seafood lovers. Do not let the words raw bar scare you away. The restaurant does offer oysters and certain seafoods served raw or undercooked for those who appreciate such delicacies, but most of their seafood dishes are cooked to taste. They serve dinner daily from 5 to 10 PM. Call 613 680 2949 to book a table.

* WILFRID'S – This elegant restaurant is the highlight of dining at the Chateau Laurier in the heart of Ottawa. The ambiance, service and quality of the dishes served lives up to the original high standards of this venerable hotel, and never waivers. In addition to their evening meal, Wilfrid's also serves elegant breakfast and lunch as well as Sunday brunch. Their hours are weekdays from 7 to 11 AM and weekends from 7 AM to 3 PM. Dinner is served Friday and Saturday between 5 and 8 PM. To book a table at Wilfrid's call 613 241 1414.

Wilfrid's at the Chateau Laurier, (Compliments of Chateau Laurier)

DESSERTS: In Canada dessert is considered to be an event but despite the strong Québécois influence, there are surprisingly few restaurants and cafes where dessert with coffee or tea is the main focus. Ottawa is well not endowed with highly recommended dessert establishments like you find in Toronto, Montréal or even many smaller cities in eastern Canada. My favorites are:

* BEAVER TAILS – The beaver tail is a local creation that is not what I would call fine gastronomy, but it is a local tradition. It is a fried confection covered in icing sugar or maple syrup generally eaten on the go. There are also savory variations on this local treat. Beaver Tails located at 69 George Street in Byward Market is one of the most visited for this truly Canadian confection. It is open Monday thru Thursday from 11 AM to 11 PM. Friday from 11 AM to Midnight, Saturday from 10 AM to Noon and Sunday from 10 AM to 11 PM. Although this is Canadian fast food, it should be tried by visitors.

* LE BOULANGERIE FRANCAIS – On 119 Murray Street near the Notre Dame Cathedral, this centrally located French style bakery and café offers both delightful pastries and light meals for take home and table service. Unfortunately they do not post their hours of service, so you will need to call 613 789 7941 before attempting to visit.

* LE MOULIN DE PROVENCE - This café and bakery is a good place for light snacks and desserts. They offer a variety of freshly baked delicacies, especially macaroons in varied flavors. They are in the Byward Market at #55 and open7 AM to 6 PM daily with closing at 7 PM on Sunday. Reservations are unnecessary.

SHOPPING

When visiting a major city like Ottawa, and for most it will be a foreign city, shopping is always an activity with widespread appeal. This holds true even for the vast number of American visitors. Most visitors are generally from the United States, and they have the advantage of the currency exchange, which in 2022 hovers around a 20 to 22 percent bonus. For visitors coming from the United Kingdom or the Eurozone, there is also a sizeable exchange bonus, which encourages you to shop.

The question many people ask is, "What is there to buy in Canada that would be special?" And for any foreign visitor that is a fair question. Most major brand products found in Canada are the same as found in the United States and Western Europe. And prices are comparable after considering the exchange rate. Goods from the United Kingdom, especially such items as wool sweaters, fine crockery and bone china and glassware are priced below what American visitors would pay at home because Canada is part of the Commonwealth. There are also Canadian brands of clothing that have their own distinctive style, the most recognized brand being Roots Canada.

When it comes to food items, the most popular is 100 percent pure maple syrup. If you are a tea drinker, then I highly recommend Red Rose Tea, as it has been a Canadian staple item for decades. And it is a high quality black tea and available in all supermarkets. If you like tinned salmon, you will find that in Canada you can buy red sockeye and Coho, which are not found in American or most European markets. The best brand is Clover Leaf, available in all Canadian super markets.

For those who love fine pastries, many who live in the United States, the one item that is popular as a take home souvenir is a box of fine pastries, especially petit fours and other fine small cakes. These are just not as widely available in the United States, especially in smaller American cities. There are so many fine bakeries or patisseries that it is not difficult for visitors who are driving to bring a box home to enjoy

Fine art is another item that is popular among those who collect paintings, carvings and other handcrafts. There is a definite style of painting ascribed to Canada, having developed in the past century by a cadre of artists known as "The Group of Seven." Their style of landscape art falls more in the category of impressionism, but with a very distinct Canadian flavor recognized globally as a unique school of art. For those not able or willing to spend thousands of dollars on an original Group of Seven painting, there are reproductions available in souvenir shops and also in some art galleries.

Here are my personal recommendations as to where to shop, displayed in this chapter by category.

CANADIAN FOODS: If you wish to purchase /Canadian food items noted above, these are my recommendations.

* **Loblaw Real Canadian Superstore** – Loblaw's is Canada's largest supermarket chain. The closest for those in downtown hotels is located at 190 Richmond Road about 3 kilometers west of the downtown core.. It is open from 7 AM to 11 PM daily.

* **Sobey's** – This is one of eastern Canada's major grocery chains. The nearest store in the downtown core is at 193 Metcalfe Street. It is open daily from 8 AM to 8 PM

DEPARTMENT STORES: Canadian cities still feature major department stores in their downtown core, something that appears to becoming rare in American cities.

* **Hudson's Bay Company Downtown Ottawa** – The most famous Canadian department store is Hudson's Bay Company, which was initially established in 1673 as a trading post serving the wild frontier. This company ultimately morphed into the popular department store chain seen today. Hudson's Bay Company in downtown Ottawa is located at 73 Rideau Street opposite the Rideau Centre and attached to it by a skyway. and is open daily from 10 AM to 8 PM. This is the only major full service department store in the downtown core.

Hudson's Bay Company Rideau Centre in Ottawa, (Work of Mario Roberto Duran Ortiz, CC BY SA 3.0, Wikimedia.org)

Nordstrom Rideau Centre, (Work of Jeangagnon, CC BY SA 4.0, Wikimedia.org)

* Nordstrom – This American high end department store does have one branch in the in the Rideau Centre in the heart of downtown Ottawa. It is open 10 AM to 8

PM daily. There are also many other fine stores in the Rideau Centre, which is also attached by skyway to the Hudson's Bay Company.

* CANADIANA: There are a few very specific shops selling products that are very representative of Canada or of various local regions, in this case of Alberta. Here are my choices for Calgary:

* Byward Market – This is the large outdoor marketplace in the heart of downtown Ottawa. It covers a few square blocks and is home to many individual shops and outdoor stalls. One product in great demand by visitors is fresh maple syrup. It is abundant in Byward Market and at the best prices in Canada. Shops are open from 9 AM to 5 PM daily. It is a must see venue in downtown Ottawa.

A portion of Byward Market, (Work of Ross Dunn. CC BY SA 2.0, Wikimedia.org)

* Roots Canada – This is a popular sportswear and outer wear brand that has become globally recognized as truly Canadian. They have three stores in greater Ottawa but the best known among visitors is located inside the Rideau Centre. Hours are 11 AM to 7 PM Monday thru Saturday and from 11 AM to 6 PM on Sunday.

CANADIAN FINE ART: My sole recommendation for buying fine quality Canadian artwork is listed below:

* **Koyman Galleries** – Located at 1771 St. Laurent Boulevard requiring either a taxi or your own transportation to reach, but a good source for contemporary works by Canadian artists. Featured are many works of art that are not astronomical in cost such as original Group of Seven paintings, but they do offer works in that recognized style, but by younger artists of today's era. The 261 1602.gallery is open Monday thru Saturday from Noon to 4 PM. You can also call for an exclusive appointment at 403.

Inside Koyman Galleries, (Compliments of the gallery)

TRIPS INTO THE COUNTRYSIDE

There is more to the Greater Ottaway Area than just seeing the city. A trip or two out into the surrounding countryside gives you a totally different picture of what there is to see in the provinces of Ontario and Québec. Ottawa is situated on the border between Canada's two major cultures. The city is a blend of the Anglo and Francophone cultures and is a blend of them both. In the countryside south of the Ottawa River, the land is gently rolling and dotted with farms and small villages that date back to the earliest Anglo settlement in the late 18th century. North of the river are the Gatineau Hills and just beyond are the Laurentian Mountains with their many intervening valleys. Here the farms and villages reflect the true nature of the French or Québécois culture. Thus drives into the countryside are so distinct in that you are essentially able to explore both the Anglo and Francophone cultures just by crossing one river.

There are two most popular visits while staying in Ottawa. The closest is to the Gatineau Park, which is immediately opposite Ottawa and extends north for around 35 kilometers. Going farther afield and spending half to a full day is a drive across the Ottawa River into rural Québec and tour the many back roads of the Laurentian Mountains, known locally as des Laurentides.

A short drive into the Gatineau Park ablaze in fall colors

There are actually more local drives, but I consider them non-specific, being without a destination. There are so many routes one can take just through the Gatineau and even more into the Laurentians that the scenic opportunities are almost endless, especially with the seasonal changes.

Overlooking the Ottawa River from within the Gatineau Park, (Work of cjuneau, CC BY SA 2.0, Wikimedia.org)

Thus when visiting Ottawa you should allow a few extra days to enjoy the beauty of the countryside on both sides of the Ottawa River. Not only will you be rewarded with two types of natural landscapes, but also with seeing and savoring the delights of two distinct Canadian cultures.

A VISIT TO GATINEAU PARK

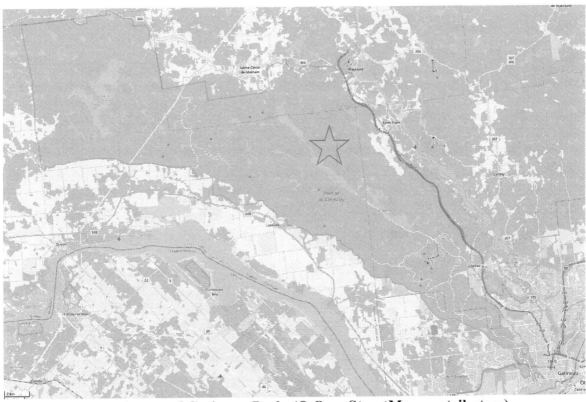

A map of Gatineau Park, (© OpenStreetMap contributors)

Gatineau Park, which begins just to the north of the Ottawa River opposite Parliament Hill and the Old Town section of Hull is a national park, but rather than being under Parks Canada, it is administered by the National Capital Commission. The park covers 361 square kilometers or 139 square miles.

Most of the parkland is a wilderness of mixed forest and dotted by many small glacial lakes. The Gatineau Hills are the geological foundation of the park. As early as the first decade of the 20th century there was talk about creating a recreational area for the national capital, but its actual creation did not occur until 1938. Today it is hard to conceive of greater Ottawa-Hull Gatineau without the park. Its creation precluded this beautiful region from becoming urbanized, as Hull and Gatineau saw the spillover of urban development in the Ottawa region.

Within the park boundaries there are portions of preexisting towns that have been allowed to remain. This has been a sore spot among those who favor maintaining a natural landscape, as there has been development of cabins and homes primarily in the small Municipality of Chelsea. If the park was part of the official national park system, it would have been better protected against such development. Among the properties that are residential, the government does maintain a small estate for use by the Prime Minister and another for the use of the Speaker of the House of Commons. But most of the land has been left in its wilderness condition with the majority of the few roads within its boundaries remaining unsealed. During the fall the park is especially magnificent, as the mixed vegetation includes a high percentage of deciduous trees that turn brilliant shades of crimson, orange, gold and yellow.

One of the true wilderness areas in Gatineau Park in fall, (Work of JonKolbert, CC BY SA 4.0, Wikimedia.org)

Gatineau Park is the oldest federally established park in Canada east of the Rocky Mountains, but unlike the other national parks of the country, it is under the jurisdiction of the National Capital Commission rather than Parks Canada.

Unlike what are recognized as national parks, the Gatineau Park is more of a day use park given that it is within the metropolitan area. So the question arises with regard what there is to do. Most people simply drive through the park and enjoy its beauty from their vehicle. And of course there are hiking or walking trails for those who want to expend some energy. The park does have 90 kilometers of trails for both hiking and cycling. And there are two designated campgrounds. Boating is popular, but only one lake allows motorized vessels.

During winter Nordic skiing is very popular with over 180 kilometers of designated trails. And there is one minor run for Alpine skiing. Most avid skiers drive farther afield to the Laurentian Mountains where the slopes are more enticing for downhill activities.

Looking toward the park's main escarpment in summer, (Work of P199, CC BY SA 3.0 Wikimedia.org)

GETTING TO GATINEAU PARK: The easiest way to visit Gatineau Park is by vehicle, but tours also offer visitors a chance to enjoy the landscapes. These are the avenues for visiting the park:

* **PRIVATE CAR** – If you have driven to Ottawa or have rented a car in the city, then you have your own transportation to the park, the lower end of which is just minutes from the downtown core. The road conditions are excellent to fair depending upon whether the road is sealed or not. Fall is the most popular time to visit because of the explosion of color in the trees.

* **CAR AND DRIVER** – Your hotel concierge can arrange a car and driver, but this is a far more expensive way to visit the park than taking a group tour, as it gives you the opportunity to set the itinerary. The services I recommend are

www.mychauffeur.com/ottawa-chauffeur-service

www.limotour.net .

* **GROUP TOURS** – There are several group tour companies, but most tend to orient their tours to within the city. These are my choices:

** Visit on line with www.grayline-ottawa.com for their listing and description of offerings.

** www.getyourgouide.com/ottawa/activities is a good source for private touring.

** Also check out www.ottawatourism.ca/ottawa-insider-guided-tours for a listing of their offerings.

Deep within the park on a back road in late fall

SPECIFIC SIGHTS TO SEE: There are only three specific places I recommend, but it is the overall drive through Gatineau Park that is the actual event when visiting.

* **MACKENZIE KING ESTATE** – This beautiful estate consisting of manicured grounds and an elegant Victorian house was once the summer home to William Lyon Mackenzie King, the longest serving prime minister of Canada from 1921 to 1930 and again from 1935 to 1948. The home and estate are in the village of Chelsea and are open 11 AM to 5 PM Monday, Wednesday and Sunday as well as from 11 AM to 8 PM on Thursday , Friday and Saturday.

* **MEECH LAKE** – Located in the middle of the park approximately 40 minutes on back roads from the center of Ottawa, this is a beautiful lake of glacial origin. Many private homes were allowed around part of the lake, thus it is not as pristine as others in the park. Because of a government conference center, the lake is an important site for high level conferences. The famous Meech Lake Accord was negotiated here, but it failed to gain full provincial support, making it one of the

notorious failures in the struggle between Canada and the Québécois in 1987 during the tense years when many Québec politicians were agitating for separation. The lake is accessible at all times, but no camping is permitted.

* SAINTE-CECILE-DE-MASHAM – This is one of the small, but very typical Québécois villages within the park. It is a classic example of the architectural style found in rural Québec and an interesting place for an afternoon stroll.

Drive north on Québec Autoroute 105, which is the expressway leading out of the Gatineau urban landscape to the north. Turn west on to Québec route 366 into the village of Sainte-Cecile-de-Masham. The total drive is 41 kilometers or 25.4 kilometers with 60 percent on dual carriage expressway.

PLACES TO DINE: There are several places where you can dine when visiting Gatineau Park, but they are all outside of the actual park boundary. My choices for lunch are:

* L'OREE du BOIS – One of the most delightful places to dine when visiting the Gatineau Park is L'Oree du Bois. The atmosphere and traditional cuisine are quintessential Québec. The menu combines many dishes of pure French origin with those classed as Québécois and you will have a difficult time deciding what to choose among their tempting choice. The restaurant is located at 15 Chemin Kingsmere in the village of Chelsea, which is just off Autoroute 105. Call 819 827 0332 to book a table.

* LE RESTO CHELSEA ; Located in the village of Chelsea at 528 Route 105 just off of Autoroute 105, this is a superb restaurant for tasting the delights of Québécois cuisine. One dish that is always on the menu is poutine, a local favorite, but one that is quite a heavy meal. Freshly made fries are topped with meat gravy and a soft white cheese – pure cholesterol but a beloved dish. Their hours are from 11:30 AM to 8 PM Tuesday and Wednesday, closing at 8:30 Thursday, Friday and Saturday. Sunday they serve only until 3 PM. Call 819 827 5559 to book a table.

* LES FOUGERES – This is one of my most favored places for a leisurely lunches when visiting Gatineau Park. It is located in the village of Tenaga just off of the Autoroute 105. I have been coming here for years.

Their menu is traditional with fine quality Canadian and French dishes. And the service is always very gracious. They are open Wednesday thru Friday from 11:30 AM to 9 PM and on weekends from 10 AM to 9:30 PM Call to book a table at 819 827 8942.

TOURING THE LAURENTIAN MOUNTAINS OF QUÉBEC

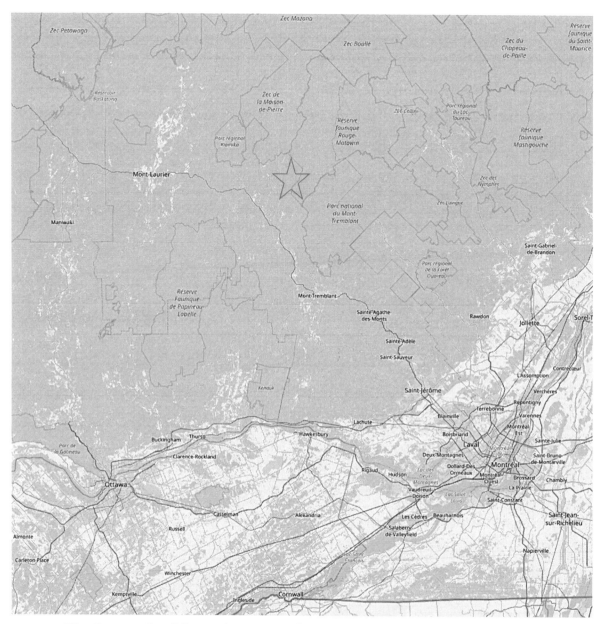

The Laurentian Mountains north of Ottawa, (© OpenStreetMap contributors)

The Laurentian Mountains are not as high or dramatic as the Canadian Rockies, but they still are a significant landform feature in the province of Québec, with their maximum elevations rising to as high as 1,666 meters or 3,825 feet, serving as a significant boundary between the gentle lowlands of the St. Lawrence River Valley. These are ancient mountains, their rock layers having been deposited in the Pre-Cambrian Era some 540,000,000 years ago, long before there was any life on earth. They Laurentians are part of a much larger collection of strata that stretch all the way across northern Canada. This collectively is known as the Canadian Shield, a land of hard rock, pockmarked by millions of lakes primarily of glacial origin. The shield has little soil but supports part of the world's largest belt of coniferous forest that not only encompasses nearly half the landmass of Canada, but also a vast portion of northern Asia. It is known as the Boreal Forest or Taiga. Most of Russia, Scandinavia, Alaska and Canada lie within this vast and unforgiving landscape. Much of the wood for construction, pulp and paper in the world comes from the Boreal Forest.

The hard ancient rock of the Canadian Shield is very rich in ferrous and non-ferrous minerals such as iron, nickel, copper, gold, silver and platinum. Such Canadian place names as Sudbury, Flin Flon, Timmins and Yellowknife represent important mining camps developed on the shield.

The Gatineau Hills just to the north of Ottawa are geologically and geographically considered to be an outlier of the Laurentians, essentially the foothills. The nearest major tourist destination within the Laurentians is Mont Tremblant, and it is 163 kilometers or 101 miles north of Ottawa. The main core of the Laurentian Mountains is to the north and west of Montréal and Ville de Québec.

GETTING TO THE LAURENTIAN MOUNTAINS: The easiest way to visit the Laurentians is by vehicle, but tours also offer visitors a chance to enjoy the landscapes. These are the avenues for visiting the park:

* PRIVATE CAR – If you have driven to Ottawa or have rented a car in the city, then you have your own transportation to the park, the lower end of which is just minutes from the downtown core. The road conditions are excellent to fair depending upon whether the road is sealed or not. Fall is the most popular time to visit because of the explosion of color in the trees. There are many alternate routes once crossing into Gatineau, some sealed and others being true backroads. The major hub for visitors is Mont Tremblant, eastern Canada's most significant ski resort. But to enjoy the mountains one does not need to venture that far from Ottawa.

* CAR AND DRIVER – Your hotel concierge can arrange a car and driver, but this is a far more expensive way to visit the park than taking a group tour, as it gives you the opportunity to set the itinerary. The services I recommend are

www.mychauffeur.com/ottawa-chauffeur-service

www.limotour.net

* GROUP TOURS – There are several group tour companies, but most tend to orient their tours to within the city. These are my choices:

** Visit on line with www.grayline-ottawa.com for their listing and description of offerings.

** www.getyourgouide.com/ottawa/activities is a good source for private touring.

The heart of the Laurentian Mountains, (© OpenStreetMap contributors)

TOURING OPTIONS: You can visit the heart of the Laurentian Mountains for the day from Ottawa or Montréal , or preferably stay overnight at the very least. This is a world class park with stunning scenery and many recreational options. For this reason I do recommend more than just a few hours on a single day visitation.

* PRIVATE VEHICLE OPTION: It is also possible to hire a car and driver for a day trip to the Laurentians, but if you plan to stay overnight or a few days, and you do not have a car at your disposal, either your own or a rental vehicle, you can arrange for a car and driver to bring you to the main town of Mont Tremblant, then have your hotel arrange another local car and driver in the park for a day or multiple day touring.

The local beauty of rural landscapes in the Laurentian Mountains

* GROUP TOURING OPTION: * GROUP TOURS – There are several group tour companies, but most tend to orient their tours to within the city of Ottawa. These are my choices for those that will take you into the Laurentians:

** Visit on line with www.grayline-ottawa.com for their listing and description of offerings.

** www.getyourgouide.com/ottawa/activities is a good source for private touring.

** Also check out www.ottawatourism.ca/ottawa-insider-guided-tours for a listing of their offerings.

SPECIFIC SIGHTS TO SEE: For the majority of day visitors coming from Ottawa just the drive to and from Mont Tremblant is the major sight. If you just on choose one road going north and then a different one coming back to Ottawa you will have more than enough scenery to provide for a superb day of sightseeing. Combine this with a nice lunch in Mont Tremblant and you will be quite satisfied.

As for routes, I recommend taking Autoroute 50 east out of Gatineau, leaving the highway on Route 315 through Buckingham. Follow Route 315 past Lac la Blanche and Montpellier, continuing on through Chénville to Namur. Then turn north on Route 323 into Mont Tremblant.

Deep into the Laurentians near Montpellier in early fall.

On your return I recommend getting onto Autoroute 117 east to Sainte Agathe des Monts. From here take Route 329 south to Morin Heights where the road meets up with Route 364 and jogs a very short distance through town before again continuing as Route 329 south to Autoroute e50, Here you turn west and follow the autoroute back into Gatineau. Then cross the Ottawa River back into central Ottawa.

Over the years I have used many variations on this route, but to do so you first of all need a highly detailed local map and then be willing to drive on several roads that either are not designated by a route number and/or are unsealed. You need to be adventurous to do so, but the rewards are superb.

* ADVENTURES PARK MONT-TREMBLANT – This is the popular recreation area adjacent to Mont Tremblant where summer sports activities such as canoeing, kayaking and woodland hiking can be arranged. This park entry is located at 586 Saint-Jovite in Mont Tremblant.

* LAC TREMBLANT – The beautiful glacial lake known as Lac Tremblant is a favored summer playground, especially for residents from nearby Montréal. Its proximity to the Village of Mont Tremblant gives residents the additional joy of good dining and shopping.

* **PARC DES CHUTES** – Located at 113 rue Pinoteau on the shores of beautiful Lac Tremblant. The area offers many hiking or walking trails and boating opportunities where you can enjoy some whitewater, falls and beautiful lakeside vistas.

Looking down upon Lac Tremblant in the fall from above Parc des Chutes, (Work of Taichi T, CC BY SA 3.0, Wikimedia.org)

* **PONTE PRUDE'HOMME** – This is an old and famously photographed covered bridge dating to 1918. It is located in the Village of Brébeuf and worth a stop or a walk through.

* **VILLAGE OF TREMBLANT** – The village of Tremblant has become eastern Canada's premier ski resort destination. There are hotels in many price ranges, including the luxury category, numerous ski runs for all levels and a plethora of shops and restaurants. It is the equivalent for the east of Whistler, the great ski resort in British Columbia. The village has a definite Alpine architectural flavor that gives it a very European atmosphere in addition to it already having the Québécois cultural matrix.

PLACES TO DINE: There are several places where you can dine when visiting the Laurentian Mountains in the area around Mont Tremblant. The main town offers numerous cafes and the larger resort hotels also serve lunch in their main dining room. My choices for lunch are:

* **La Sandwicherie Café ' Bistro** – This nice eatery is located at 1918 Chemin du Village Secteur vieux-village Tremblant. You will no doubt need to ask someone on the street to help you find it, as the Québécois French language does dominate and

there are few signs in English. This is a small café that serves outstanding soups and sandwiches to please all tastes. It is popular with the local populace. Their hours are from 8 AM to 4 PM daily with extended closing at 5 PM on Saturday. You do not need to reserve a table.

Mont Tremblant in fall, (Work of Taichi T, CC BY SA 4.0, Wikimedia.org)

* Restaurant La Quintessence – Located at 3004 chemin de la Chapelle Mont-Tremblant, which no doubt will necessitate your asking someone to help direct you. The restaurant is part of the Hotel Quintessence Tremblant Sur le Lac. The atmosphere and cuisine are truly representative of the Québécois culture and as a visitor this will give you a feel for rural Québec. No hours are posted on their website. Call 819 425 3400 to see if you would need to book a table during normal lunch hours.

FINAL NOTE: There are many small cafes and bistros in Mont Tremblant as well as in the other communities you will pass through en route to Mont Tremblant. Given the strong penchant in Québec for quality when it comes to dining, you almost cannot go wrong. If you like the looks of a restaurant or café you see along the way, you will in all likelihood have a good lunch.

FINAL WRAP

Ottawa is a grand capital city even though it was not initially planned for that purpose. At the time it was chosen to become Canada's capital. The original creation of Bytown was in conjunction with the completion of the Rideau Canal that would make water transit between Toronto and Montréal safe and efficient in contrast to navigating the St. Lawrence River where there was the danger of conflict with the United States, especially in the immediate aftermath of the American Civil War when British and American relationships were strained.

The honor of selecting a site for a new national capital was given to Her Majesty, Queen Victoria. It is assumed she had advice from her government ministers. The site she chose was that of Ottawa. And then the government chose the prominent bluff overlooking the Ottawa River to be the site for the national parliament buildings.

Rural Québec villages are a stone's throw from Ottawa

Ottawa has served as the national capital for the creation of Canada on July 1, 1867. It proudly serves the world's second largest nation in physical size from its location on the border between Ontario and Québec, thus providing for a degree of cultural and political unity between the two major cultures of Canada. Ontario is the most populous of Canada's ten provinces and Québec is the second most populous. Today approximately 1,500,000 people in the greater Ottawa region represent percentage wise approximately the same ratio of English versus French speaking people as does the entire nation. And many government ministries have their offices spread between the main city of Ottawa and its suburban neighbor of Hull-Gatineau, which today is normally just referred to as Gatineau.

For the visitor there is a lot to see in and around Ottawa. And the various venues are both cultural and natural. The Gatineau Hills, which are a part of the greater Laurentian Mountains offer beautiful scenery and a variety of recreational opportunities.

My final recommendation is for anyone planning to visit Ottawa to stay for at least four to five days to fully appreciate all is has to offer. And if Montréal is not on your itinerary, then you should consider adding another day to your Ottawa visit and use that day to visit Montréal by train to at least catch a glimpse of Canada's second greatest city.

Ottawa is the perfect bridge between Anglo and Francophone Canada. It is a city to be savored and enjoyed.

ABOUT THE AUTHOR

Dr. Lew Deitch

I am Canadian and a semi-retired professor of geography with over 46 years of teaching experience. During my distinguished career, I directed the Honors Program at Northern Arizona University and developed many programs relating to the study of contemporary world affairs. I also served as a professor at Simon Fraser University in Burnaby, British Columbia and spent two years in Australia as a visiting professor at the University of New England in Armidale New South Wales and Flinders University in Adelaide, South Australia

I am an honors graduate of The University of California, Los Angeles, earned my Master of Arts at The University of Arizona and completed my doctorate in geography at The University of New England in Australia. I am a globetrotter, having visited 96 countries on all continents except Antarctica. My primary focus is upon human landscapes, especially such topics as local architecture, foods, clothing and folk music. I am also a student of world politics and conflict.

I enjoy being in front of an audience, and have spoken to thousands of people at civic and professional organizations. I have been lecturing on board cruise ships for a major five star cruise line since 2008. I love to introduce people to exciting new places both by means of presenting vividly illustrated talks and through serving as a tour consultant for ports of call. I am also an avid writer, and for years I have written my own text books used in my university classes. Now I have turned my attention to writing travel companions, books that will introduce you to countries and cities you may wish to visit, but not serving as a touring book like the major guides you find in all of the bookstores.

 I also love languages, and my skills include a conversational knowledge of German, Russian and Spanish.

Arizona has been his permanent home since 1974. I presently live just outside of Phoenix in the beautiful resort city of Scottsdale and still offer a few courses for the local community colleges when I am at home.

I would like to extend an invitation for you to join me on one of the Silversea cruise segments when I am on board presenting my destination talks. You would find it to be a wonderful experience, especially after having read my book on this area, or on the others I have written about.

**TO CONTACT ME, PLEASE CHECK OUT MY WEB PAGE
FOR MORE INFORMATION AT:**
http://www.doctorlew.com

Made in United States
Orlando, FL
28 May 2022